Contents

Introduction

by

Bernard Farrell

Occasionally, I am asked how long it takes me to write a play. This question often comes from the sheer embarrassment of not knowing what to say after the introduction. But it's a good question—and a lot better than the lady who, on hearing my occupation, thought long and hard and then asked: "When you write a play, do you use a pen or a pencil?"

(I know how she felt. I was once suddenly introduced to a neurosurgeon and all I could think to ask him was: "Do you have very steady hands?")

The polite answer to how-long-it-takes-me is "nine months". The more impolite reply is "all my life". But it is also more truthful—simply because once the inspirational fuse has been lit and the play is at the planning stage, you immediately rocket back through the years. And on the way, you plunder not only your own life but the lives of everyone you've ever met (or even heard about) since you climbed out of the cradle.

All The Way Back, then, is most certainly an "all my life" play.

I clearly remember the lighting of the fuse for this one—and very embarrassing it was too. I was walking through Dun Laoghaire when a middle-aged man loomed up in front of me, spoke my name, shook my hand and became almost too emotional at seeing me again. I was certain I had never seen him before in my life!

However, his enthusiasm was infectious—and soon I too was laughing wildly, thumping his shoulder, hearing his stories and occasionally asking him vague, probing questions like: "And tell me, are you still living in the same place?"

I knew that I was quickly reaching the point of no return. After some minutes of such intimacy, it becomes impossible to say: "And by the way, who the hell are you?" But, at that moment, two things happened: I remembered exactly who he was, and I heard him say: "Did you know that I was made redundant last year?"

Sometimes a chance remark can ring a bell. Sometimes this is just a tinkle (worthy of a reminder in a notebook and no more). Sometimes it is an alarm-clock rattle (worthy of pages of notes plus, maybe, dialogue). But this, for reasons I didn't know yet, produced a clarion akin to Christ Church on New Year's Eve.

I asked him if he had time to spare. He said that these days he had all the time in the world—so we went into the Shopping Centre to begin drinking coffee.

He continued his story—how at the age of 42 he found himself both unemployed and too old to be re-employed, how his marriage suffered, how his friends disappeared, how his children first sympathised with him and then despised him. And how, recently, himself and his wife began to think of building-on something to the side of the house and maybe opening a little bakery there....."to see how it goes anyway".

I don't know how many coffees we had—but I do know that when we stood up to leave, I was already planning a play.

It wasn't, I am certain, just the story I had heard—but rather the story in relation to the background to this man that had moved me so much. As I walked away, I wanted to abandon all present work and begin the play at once. (An impulse that should always be resisted: after ten pages of furious dialogue, you suddenly realise that you don't know where you're going—and where you've been wasn't worth the trip!)

I had been at school with him. He was the one who, delirious at passing Latin, flung his books through the second-storey window—thinking it was open! He was the one who, when I broke a bone in my ankle, put me on his crossbar to take me to hospital—but crashed into the kerb on the way and broke a second bone! He was the one who, at our first Past Pupils Reunion, arrived in the white MG, smoking cigars—and said that in five years he'd be back to buy the school and turn it into a casino!

He was the one we all knew would succeed—he was the one who was unforgettable. Now, he was the one who was old beyond his years and forgotten.

I then began to realise that certain aspects of my life paralleled his—and slowly discovered why the bells had rung in my subconscious.

Some six years previously, I had left my sound, pensionable job at Sealink—and left with the genuine good wishes of my friends and colleagues. But my right hand can still turn to ice as I remember one particular hand-shake and the voice that said: "I wish you good luck—but I think you are making a dreadful mistake!" I can still recall how I laughed...in sheer terror.

There were many other terrors further back into my life to draw from—and, at that moment, a new one that had me tossing and turning late into the night. We were in the process of buying a new house and I was dealing with workmen who spoke the strange language of Builderese—which seemed to be saying that due to "availability problems" my wife and I could be spending the winter sleeping under the stars!

Then there were the memories from the notebooks: my days on the rugby field and at the rugby dances, my days spent in the employ of Estate Agents—and a remark that my family had generously made (and re-made many times) that there must be a play to be written about Hairdressing Salons.

(Not for a moment, of course, am I suggesting that my builders resembled Bimbo and Davis in the play—no more than the play's rugby stories relate to my own experiences. As ever, the immediate suggestion of a character or a circumstance is but the starting point—ready for the next stage of merging with as many plundered experiences!)

As I gathered the material, a set was already being constructed in my mind—and I began to realise that, within the play, I would commit the thrilling crime of allowing the audience to relish the interior of the house— and then see it smashed to pieces before their eyes. But I still didn't know *how*.

(An old friend recently told me that I had displayed this destructive streak years ago when, on passing the China Showrooms, I had said: "Wouldn't it be great to get in there with a hurley stick!" However, I violently deny that I ever said such a thing.)

The developing hope now was that, in the play, as the set was destroyed and re-constructed, so the lives of the characters would enter destruction and search for re-construction. And it was now clear that the basic theme would be Redundancy, that we would be dealing with a family of five people...but, after that, who or what else?

In the months that followed—while I planned to get married and, at the same time, took a crash course in Builderese (and Plumberese and Carpenterese), a new aspect of the play emerged. A title, *All The Way Back*, suggested itself—and I knew that this rugby chant would not only reflect the fight-back to survival, but would also determine the middle-class social standing of the family.

Redundancy was already becoming the economic cancer in Ireland. It attacked rich and poor alike. Both suffered by it. But, in dramatic terms, I sought the greater fall from grace to allow me to examine not just the loss of income, but the unprecedented loss of status, reputation, respect and dignity.

(Having, in the past, examined the emergence of the Nouveau Riche, perhaps I now felt it was time to explore the plight of the New Poor).

I had now sketched in some of the support characters—and I was talking to Joe Dowling of the Abbey Theatre about my general ideas. As with previous Abbey plays, he never probed too deeply at this stage (knowing,

I'm sure, that the playwright only really discovers the play for himself when he begins to write it), but he said the appropriate, encouraging things.

The actual writing of the play took nine months—helped enormously at one dreadfully blocked point by Christopher Fitz-Simon, the Abbey's Script Editor, who invited me to his home in Monkstown and in the summer heat of his conservatory, gently made some key suggestions that had me almost cheering with delight and galloping off home again—and back to the pen. (Or was it the pencil!)

In Hollywood films, there is a stock image of the playwright finishing a play. It's usually a "he"—with the tie pulled loose, the cigarette in the mouth, the glass of whiskey on the typewriter, a sheaf of completed pages beside him and one still in the typewriter on which he types "The End".

The next scene is always the razz-a-ma-tazz of the First Night!

Oh, would that it were so. In real life, the First Night never follows the writing of the play. What follows the writing of the play is the re-writing of the play!

And so, in late 1984, I was working with the play's director, Ben Barnes—who, happily, also felt thrilled by the destructive/re-constructive elements of the play. (A man for the China Showrooms perhaps?). And for weeks, we argued and agreed, became foes and friends as we tested the script to make the characters clear, the structure sound and everything ready to be rolled onto the rehearsal floor.

Any First Night carries its own terrors. But if you are in the business, you accept the rules. And that means that, after three hours have passed in a darkened auditorium, you may be loved or loathed, be declared a wizard or a wash-out, become the flavour-of-the-month or the poison-of-the-year. Whatever the outcome, you always give it your best shot...and then start praying or pulling wish-bones or both!

However, as this First Night approached, a new terror was introduced. For this was (yet again) a time in theatrical history when the Abbey was declared to be in difficulties. Once again, the black wreath was about to be hung on the door, the death-knell was ready to be sounded. And the cry went out: "Will Bernard Farrell's play save the Abbey?" It was a pressure that Ben and I tried to resist, but couldn't ignore.

On all First Nights, I become like a duck: I stay calm above the surface but paddle like the devil underneath. On this First Night, I was so calm that I think people were beginning to worry about me. But everything else in my entire system was paddling like a Mississippi steamer out of control!

I can now look back happily to that première, to the play's success and to its run. And, with more relaxed happiness, to its even more successful revival at the Abbey in the summer of 1985. By then, I had got married, the house was ready, we had moved to Greystones and I was already planning a new play—also, in time, to be directed by Ben Barnes at the Abbey.

Plays are seldom declared to be finished. Unlike the Hollywood stereotype (who'd be in a hammock in the Bahamas at this point!) I was, years later, still benefitting from seeing subsequent productions of the play—and the generous suggestions of directors such as Ben (yet again) and Gerry Barnes in professional presentations and Margaret Dunne in the amateur arena. The present script incorporates all that I (eventually) agreed with...with my thanks.

One memory of the First Night remains. I had got tickets for an old friend and, after the show, he loomed up in front of me and told me how much he had enjoyed it. And amid all the theatrical talk around me, we remembered our countless coffees in the Shopping Centre years before—and I knew then that the play had been written for him.

All The Way Back

This play was first produced at the Abbey Theatre, Dublin, on 14 March, 1985, with the following cast.

Brendan Ryan	Clive Geraghty
Sheila Ryan	Máire O'Neill
Paul Ryan	Sean Campion
Mary Ryan	Maeve Germaine
Michael Ryan	Barry Lynch
Catherine Ryan	Joan O'Hara
Mr. Mulligan	Dónall Farmer
Mr. Davis	Tom Hickey
Bimbo	Donagh Deeney
Bill Patterson	Emmet Bergin
Miss Quinn	Jill Doyle
Mrs. O'Sullivan	Lucy Vigne Welsh
Mrs. Prendergast	Kathleen Barrington
Mrs. Brophy	May Cluskey

The play was directed by Ben Barnes and designed by Wendy Shea. Lighting by Leslie Scott.

ACT ONE

Scene One

The open-plan lounge/dining room of Ryan's house. (If space is limited in production, the dining area may be off SL.) In the SR wall is a panoramic window. Beyond the lounge back wall is the garage (revealed in Act 2). A short corridor to front door at SL back. A downstairs toilet here and also the stairs. Off SL is the kitchen, etc. The house is tastefully furnished. However, there are too many identical table lamps. Some crutches and various orthopaedic appliances scattered about. Photographs of rugby teams on the walls. A trophy cabinet of cups and statuettes against the back wall. An international cap hanging above it. Also here: a drinks cabinet, a stereo unit, a telephone and a bookcase.

At rise of curtain, MICHAEL RYAN is moving the Trophy Cabinet an inch or two. He then takes a long folding rule from his pocket to measure the back wall. He is 20, very well groomed. CATHERINE RYAN, aged 53, comes quietly down the stairs. She is a rather furtive woman—with airs of grandeur. She now carries some books, a magazine and a pen.

It is 5.00 p.m. The month is March.

CATHERINE: Anyone home? (*Pause*). I repeat—anyone home?

MICHAEL: (*Guiltily*) Yes, Aunt Catherine. I'm here—in the lounge. (*Hides the rule*) I was just in the lounge.

CATHERINE: (*Suspiciously*) What's going on now?

MICHAEL: Going on now?

CATHERINE: Yes, going on now—there's something very peculiar going on in this house lately.

MICHAEL: Something very peculiar?

CATHERINE: A lot of creeping around and whispering.

MICHAEL: Creeping around and whispering?

CATHERINE: And making plans of some kind...

MICHAEL: Making plans?

CATHERINE: Do you have to repeat everything like a parrot?

MICHAEL: Like a parrot?

CATHERINE: Oh yes, Michael, act the fool if you wish—but I know there is something going on here. I'm well aware of all the

10

whispers...and all the silences too. (*Waits. Silence*) Silences like this one.

MICHAEL: Oh, this silence is because they're all out: Dad is at his interview, Mum is still at the supermarket, Mary went with her because the car wouldn't start and Paul won't be in from the bank until after six. So they're all...out and about.

CATHERINE: And Mr. Mulligan—is he also "out and about"?

MICHAEL: No, I forgot—he came back and went into that toilet.

CATHERINE: I want him to help me with a question in this competition.

MICHAEL: With three artificial legs. (*Amused*)

CATHERINE: I beg your pardon?

MICHAEL: He came back and went into the toilet with three artificial legs...and that was over half an hour ago.

CATHERINE: Michael, what Mr. Mulligan does in the privacy of the toilet—with or without his three artificial legs—need not concern us in the slightest. I merely want to consult him on this competition—the prize is a fourteen-day tour of the Isle of Man.

MICHAEL: Dad says he tries them on in there.

CATHERINE: Tries what on in there?

MICHAEL: All his artificial legs.

CATHERINE: And how on earth can he try on artificial legs if he has two real legs of his own?

MICHAEL: But has he? Dad says that if you listen carefully, you can hear him sort of squeak every time he walks or sits or bends or...

CATHERINE: (*Angrily*) Your father would be better off finding himself a respectable job.

MICHAEL: (*Indicates*) He brought those in as well—surgical boots and crutches.

CATHERINE: Is that a carpenters' rule you are holding?

MICHAEL: This? Well...well, yes, I was just...

CATHERINE: I sincerely hope you are not considering a trade as a career?

MICHAEL: No—I'm already trained as a hairdresser, Aunt Catherine.

CATHERINE: Oh yes. Of course. To be like your mother—the Cabra Hairdresser—who always believed that scrubbing people's heads was something to be proud of. Tell Mr. Mulligan I will speak with him later. (*Goes upstairs*)

MICHAEL: Okay, Aunt Catherine.

CATHERINE: And tell your mother that when dinner is ready, she may sound the gong. I will be in my room.

MICHAEL: (*Quietly*) We don't have a gong, Aunt Catherine.

MICHAEL *begins again to measure the back wall. The hall door opens.* BRENDAN RYAN, *aged 50, well-dressed, carrying a briefcase, enters.*

BRENDAN: (*Calls*) Sheila? I'm home. (MICHAEL *stops and waits nervously.*) Sheila? (*Takes off his coat. Angrily to himself*) "Actually we're looking for a younger man." Next they'll want us in Pampers nappies and munching Farley's Rusks before they'll even give a bloody interview. (*Comes into the lounge*) Ah, Michael—where's your mother?

MICHAEL: She's still at the supermarket, Dad. How did the interview go?

BRENDAN: She couldn't be still at the supermarket—the car's outside.

MICHAEL: She didn't take it, Dad, because it wouldn't start. I think the damp got into the choke.

BRENDAN: Into the plugs. And why didn't she ring the AA? That's what we pay our subscription for.

MICHAEL: She said it wasn't paid.

BRENDAN: (*Stops.*) Oh. (*Pause.*) Well, she should have phoned them anyway—(*Looks through the post*) Probably something very simple...

MICHAEL: Probably just the damp got into the choke.

BRENDAN: (*Angrily*) The damp doesn't get into the choke!—it gets into the plugs or into the Distributor Cap, not into the choke! And if you spent less time reading those fashion magazines, you'd know that. Is this all the post that came?

MICHAEL: And some puzzles for Aunt Catherine.

BRENDAN: (*Looks at the envelopes*) Look: brown, brown, brown, brown...This must be a mistake: a white envelope! (*Opens it.*)

MICHAEL: I got no replies at all to the ads I answered—not even from salons that would let me wash and blow-dry.

BRENDAN: Wash and blow-dry! There's no future in washing and blow-drying women's hair. If you'd got into playing rugby, like I told you, you'd have got the contacts...you'd be in the bank the same as Paul is...or in your own business. (*Of the letter*) Now this is what I'm talking about—contacts. This is from Bill Patterson, my old rugby mate. (*Reads.*)

MICHAEL: (*Pause*) How did the interview go today?

BRENDAN: Listen to this—he'd like me to captain the golf tour to Royal Portrush in August! That's what I mean by contacts, Michael. I haven't seen Bill for months and we only played one international game together, thirty years ago, but the bond remains. I wouldn't get that if I was washing and blow-drying...(*Reads.*)

MICHAEL: Was today's interview alright, Dad?

BRENDAN: What? The interview? Oh, very good—very positive reaction. (*Of the letter*) And a P.S.—"Helen and I are thinking of taking your advice and making it Barbados this year." We recommended that.

MICHAEL: Did they say they'd phone or what?

BRENDAN: Phone? But Bill and Helen only live across the...

MICHAEL: No, the people that interviewed you—did they say they'd phone?

BRENDAN: Oh them—yes. Yes, they'll be on to me alright. Went very well. Very positive reaction. What time is it now?

MICHAEL: Gone five-thirty.

BRENDAN: Two-thirty to five-thirty—time to take out the contact lenses—this one is beginning to feel as though it's glued to my eyeball. Next week, four hours. (*Goes towards the toilet.*) Is Catherine in?

MICHAEL: (*Quickly, as* BRENDAN *reaches the door*) Yes—but Mr. Mulligan is still locked in that toilet.

BRENDAN: Oh, holy Christ, not again! (*Rattles the door handle*) Hello! Hello!

MULLIGAN: (*Off*) Sorry—it's engaged.

BRENDAN: (*Loudly*) Mr. Mulligan, this is Mr. Ryan!

MULLIGAN: (*Off*) Sorry, Mr. Ryan—just a moment.

BRENDAN: (*Angrily*) Thank you very much. (*To* MICHAEL) It's gone beyond a joke with that bloody lodger locking himself in the toilets—if it isn't that one he's stuck in, it's the other one. Get up for a quiet pee at any hour of the bloody night and there he is—"Just a moment..."

MULLIGAN: (*Off*) Just a moment.

BRENDAN: (*Angrily*) Thank you!

MICHAEL: He has three artificial legs in there with him...

BRENDAN: He has artificial arms and legs all over the house—it's like the bloody Chamber of Horrors here every morning. Where in the name of God did Sheila get him from!
The front door opens. SHEILA—*aged 46 and attractive—comes in. She struggles with many Dunne's stores bags.*

SHEILA: Oh hello, Brendan—I hope you're not waiting for your dinner.

BRENDAN: (*Angrily*) I'm waiting for your bloody lodger to get out of this toilet.

SHEILA: (*Angrily*) Brendan! He'll hear you!

BRENDAN: Let him hear me—in there playing with his peg-leg!

SHEILA: And why don't you use the toilet upstairs?

BRENDAN: Because, Sheila, I happen to be the owner of this house and

13

he happens to be the lodger.

SHEILA: (*Angrily*) Oh right! I take it from that, that the interview didn't go well.

BRENDAN: (*Angrily*) The interview has nothing to do with it. The interview went bloody great as a matter of fact—they're just dying to give me the job.

SHEILA: (*Angrily*) Well that's wonderful news—that's the end of all our worries, isn't it? Michael, why are you standing there?—run out and help Mary, and don't annoy her any further. No sense in having the whole family behaving like lunatics.

MICHAEL: Right, Mum. (*Runs out.*)

BRENDAN: (*Helps Sheila. Quietly*) Sorry about that, Sheila—it's these contact lenses: this one's like a needle in my eye. And sorry about the car...

SHEILA: (*Quietly*) Doesn't matter. Michael said it was probably just the damp got into the choke.

BRENDAN: (*Controlled*) Yes, probably! But if I'd remembered the AA subscription...

SHEILA: It's alright, the bus stopped right outside the supermarket—but don't mention it to Mary. Bobby Collins saw her carrying the potatoes and said that her arms were getting so long, she'd soon look like a baboon. So don't mention supermarkets to her.

BRENDAN: (*Laughs*) Or baboons, I suppose?

SHEILA: (*Laughs*) Yes, or baboons. (*Pause*) How was the interview?

BRENDAN: As usual it was grand—until they got to my age. They said they expected a younger man...and there were 85 others in for the job.

SHEILA: Oh.

BRENDAN: But they did say they'd ring me.

SHEILA: Well, there's hope...we can only wait and see.

BRENDAN: Yes. (*Brightly*) And we're bound to strike it rich some time.

SHEILA: Of course we are. I'll put these inside...(*Goes into the kitchen.*) MR MULLIGAN *comes from the toilet. He is 52, thin and undernourished. He carries three artificial legs.*

BRENDAN: Ah, Mr. Mulligan. I hope I didn't interrupt...whatever you were doing.

MULLIGAN: No, no—I was just washing my legs in the sink. It's a new type of plastic I'm hoping will sell very well.

BRENDAN: Must make you feel like a centipede sometimes—washing all your legs.

MULLIGAN: Oh, not just legs—I have arms, ankles, elbows, hip-joints and two hundred knee-caps and a lovely new hand-and-wrist:

great flexibility and movement—a surgeon friend of mine is really keen on them.

BRENDAN: Great. Now, if you'll excuse me—I must take this out. (*Indicating his eye*)

MULLIGAN: I didn't know you had a glass eye!

BRENDAN: I don't have a glass eye! I have contact lenses.

MULLIGAN: Oh sorry—force of habit. I also deal in glass eyes and plastic ears and...And I trust you had a satisfactory interview?

BRENDAN: (*Stops*) I beg your pardon?

MULLIGAN: Did you have a satisfactory interview today?

BRENDAN: (*Coldly*) I had a very satisfactory interview, thank you. However, it is really of little importance to me as I'll soon be going back into private business myself.

MULLIGAN: More table lamps?

BRENDAN: Something similar, yes. Anything else?

MULLIGAN: No, no. I said a prayer for you.

BRENDAN: (*Stops*) I beg your pardon?

MULLIGAN: I'm a great believer in prayer, Mr. Ryan, because in my business—in my *other* business, that is, before my unfortunate mistake with the you know what—I've seen people lose a lot more than their jobs...

BRENDAN: I haven't lost my job, Mr. Mulligan...

MULLIGAN: ...I've seen them lose arms, legs, lips, even little intimate organs—and now, in my present business, I can say to them "lose what you like, say your prayers, and I'll fix you up—as long as you don't lose the 'oul head". (*Laughs*) A little joke, Mr. Ryan. "As long as you don't lose the 'oul head."

BRENDAN: (*Coldly*) Excuse me. (*Goes into the toilet*)
SHEILA *comes from the kitchen.*

MULLIGAN: Oh Mrs. Ryan—I've volunteered to ring the Angelus at six...

SHEILA: That's fine, Mr. Mulligan—dinner will be late anyway...

MULLIGAN: The sacristan is still wearing the spinal support I sold him and his legs go numb every time he pulls the rope.
MICHAEL *comes in carrying some Dunne's bags.*

MICHAEL: Mary's bringing in more, Mummy...

SHEILA: Thanks Michael—I've turned the cooker on, if you'll keep an eye on it. (*Goes upstairs*)

MULLIGAN: Hello again, Michael. (*Goes into the lounge*)

MICHAEL: Hello, Mr. Mulligan. (*Pauses to listen for a squeak as* MULLIGAN *walks away. Then goes into the kitchen*)
BRENDAN *comes in from the toilet. He now wears glasses.*

15

BRENDAN: (*Brightly*) There we are, Mr. Mulligan—vacant again—if you want to wash your two hundred knee-caps.

MULLIGAN: No, no—a bit of bookwork now before my hospital visits tomorrow. (*Laughs*) I'm a man of many parts, Mr. Ryan.

BRENDAN: That's what we all suspect, Mr. Mulligan.

MARY *comes in. She is 15, wears a school uniform, carries two bags. She looks dejected.*

BRENDAN: Ah Mary, I see you were at the super...(*Remembers*) I hear you were at school today.

MARY: I'm at school every day, Daddy. How did your interview go?

BRENDAN: My interview? Now, don't you be worrying about my interview—today's was very good, very positive. But more important, how did your Geography exam go?

MARY: Rotten. Everyone said it was rotten. Rita O'Reilly took one look at the paper and vomited all over Sister Monica's feet. Sister Monica said that if she did that again, she'd be expelled.

BRENDAN: Quite right too—otherwise you'd all be at it.

MARY: And then I had to go to the supermarket because the car wouldn't start.

BRENDAN: Oh really?

MARY: Michael said it was the damp that got into the choke.

BRENDAN: (*Quietly*) Good God!

MARY: (*Stands—hands hanging loosely by her sides*) Dad, do you notice anything about me?

BRENDAN: Notice anything? (*Awkwardly*) Notice anything like what?

MARY: Like anything. (*Hangs her hands longer*) When I stand like this.

BRENDAN: Well, I notice you look smashing—that's what I notice.

MARY: But my arms.

BRENDAN: Your arms? What about your arms?

MARY: Where they come to. Look.

BRENDAN: But that's all right. That's normal. Everyone's arms come to there. Look at mine. Look where they come to. See—perfectly normal.

MULLIGAN: Perfectly normal.

MARY: Bobby Collins says mine are as long as a monkey's.

BRENDAN: I bet he doesn't say that when he has you on the back of his motor-bike, holding onto him.

MARY: Oh, don't you think he looks like Heathcliff with his hair blowing back and...

BRENDAN: I think he should wear a crash-helmet—the same as yours.

MARY: But that's his I wear—he gave it to me. I'm glad you like him...(*Kisses him*)...and I really hope you get a job soon again...

BRENDAN: Don't you be worrying about me getting a job...
> SHEILA *comes down the stairs. She has changed her clothes.*
SHEILA: Mary, would you change out of that uniform now—we don't
> want to be all sitting around waiting while you parade in front of a
> mirror up there.
MARY: (*Testily*) All right! (*Goes upstairs.*)
SHEILA: Brendan, I left your jogging shorts in the airing cabinet.
BRENDAN: Oh great. I'm meeting the lads at seven—three miles, flat
> out, is the target.
> (*The phone rings*)
BRENDAN: (*Into phone*) Brendan Ryan speaking.
> MICHAEL *comes quickly from the kitchen.*
SHEILA: (*To* MICHAEL) It's all right.
BRENDAN: (*Into phone*) Oh, that's very kind of you—well anything you
> want to ask me, I'll be more than happy to...
MICHAEL: (*Quietly to* SHEILA) Is it from today's interview?
SHEILA: (*To* MICHAEL) Couldn't be...
BRENDAN: (*Into phone*) Well, let's see—I had the exclusive European
> agency for all their goods and, in 1979, *Business and Finance* voted
> us the top...(*Listens*)
MICHAEL: (*To* SHEILA) He told me that today's went very well.
SHEILA: (*Sadly*) When did he ever tell you anything else?
BRENDAN: (*Into phone*) Well, I thought I gave you all those details in
> my application...
MULLIGAN: Five-to, Mrs. Ryan—I'm off.
SHEILA: Pardon? Oh, very well, Mr. Mulligan. We'll see you after your
> Angelus.
MULLIGAN: (*Goes towards the door*) And I'll tidy up all those crutches
> when I get back. (*Goes*)
BRENDAN: (*Into phone*) Did I not mention my age at all?
SHEILA: Oh God...
BRENDAN: (*Forced cheerfulness*) Oh, I'm so sorry. Well, to put the
> record straight then—as we used to say on the cricket field—I'm
> batting at the old half-century.
SHEILA: (*Quietly*) God...just tell them!
BRENDAN: (*Into phone*) Well, what batting at the old half-century
> means, is that I'm...I'm fifty. Well, that's just fifty—last February,
> in fact...so really just over the forty-nine mark...
SHEILA: (*Quietly*) This is terrible...
BRENDAN: (*Brightly into phone*) Well yes, I know the age limit in your
> advertisement—but I would maintain that experience is...(*Pause*).
> Oh yes, I quite see that point too.

MICHAEL: (*To* SHEILA) Did you tell him anything about what we're doing tomorrow?

SHEILA: (*Sharply*) No, I did not—and I hope that you didn't either.

MICHAEL: I didn't—but I think Aunt Catherine suspects something. She was asking me...

SHEILA: Let her suspect all she likes. It's none of her business.

BRENDAN: (*Into phone*) Fine—and I'd be happy to see you too first thing tomorrow morning...

SHEILA: (*To* MICHAEL) Look in at that dinner—it's another interview. (*Goes to drinks cabinet. Pours two sherries.*)

MICHAEL: Okay, Mum. (*Goes into kitchen.*)

BRENDAN: (*Into phone*) Excellent—so I'll see you at nine-thirty in the morning and thank you very much for...(*They are gone. Slams down the phone*) Well, that's another bloody mistake: not putting my age on applications. That's what comes of that!

SHEILA: But they are giving you an interview, aren't they?

BRENDAN: They said they'd see me! I should have said if they only wanted to see me, I could walk past their window and they could give me the fingers from there.

SHEILA: (*Gives him a sherry*) I'd have thought that not putting your age on the application would have allowed them to assess you without...

BRENDAN: Well, obviously it doesn't work that way, does it? And those contact lenses don't work either.

SHEILA: They do make you look young and that is very important if...

BRENDAN: They make me look a lot of things. In the middle of today's interview—just as I was spoofing that I played for Ireland *thirty* years ago—something got into one of them and the chairman thought I was bloody winking at him. No wonder he didn't even shake hands with me—probably thought to himself: "this isn't just an old, washed-up, redundant executive—this is an old, washed-up, redundant, executive queen!"

SHEILA: Now Brendan, talking like that is...

BRENDAN: And now peg-leg Mulligan says that he's praying for me. That's the last bloody straw. (*The Angelus is heard ringing*) No, it's not—he's probably ringing that Angelus for me too.

SHEILA: He's been through it all too, Brendan—he was made redundant...

BRENDAN: (*Angrily*) Redundant from what? What was he up to—hacking away at people.

SHEILA: He was out of work, Brendan, no matter what he was doing—and he got back on his feet again and...

BRENDAN: (*Angrily*) Well God knows he has enough feet to get back on—he has this house littered with arms, legs and feet—squeaking around the house all day, dropping them everywhere. (*Stops*) I'm sorry, Sheila—today's interview was bloody awful. They said I was too old...and tomorrow I'll be a day older. It's bloody hopeless. *The hall door opens.* PAUL *comes in. He is 22, very smartly dressed in a suit. His left wrist is in a simple sling.*

SHEILA: Oh Paul! What time is it? I hope you're not in a hurry for your dinner...

PAUL: (*Stops*) Are you joking! I told you this morning—I'm taking Judy to the Elton John concert.

SHEILA: Paul, I forgot all about that...

PAUL: But it was the last thing I said going out this morning.

SHEILA: It's alright Paul—it'll be ready in a minute.

PAUL: Good God!—it isn't as if you're all out working all day.

BRENDAN: Alright, Paul! The dinner is late because the car wouldn't start...

SHEILA: Your father thinks it was damp got into the choke...

PAUL: How could damp get into the choke!

BRENDAN: (*Furiously*) I didn't say that!

PAUL: Well, when will dinner be ready? Judy will hit the shaggin' roof.

SHEILA: I'll tell Michael you're in, Paul. (*Goes quickly into the kitchen.*)

PAUL: (*Quietly*) Everyone hanging around the house, talking rubbish ...about damp in the choke! I'd better phone her and tell her.

BRENDAN: It's been a trying day for your mother, Paul.

PAUL: (*Dials*) The bank isn't exactly a holiday camp, Dad.

BRENDAN: I know. (*Pause*) How's the rugby injury? Tingling a bit, I'd say.

PAUL: It's fine. (*Slams the phone down*) Damn! Engaged!

BRENDAN: Have they taken you off the cash counter?

PAUL: Yes, I'm back to Accounts. How did today's interview go?

BRENDAN: Oh, very good. Very positive reaction. And another one in the morning. Feel very positive about that.

SHEILA: (*Comes from the kitchen*) Soup in five minutes, Paul.

PAUL: (*Dials again*) Great. Thanks.

SHEILA: Are you off the cash counter with your injury?

PAUL *loses the number. Angrily dials again.*

BRENDAN: He's back to accounts—nursing the limb. (*To* PAUL) Did I ever tell you, Paul, about the injury I got in my game against...

PAUL/BRENDAN: Wales at Cardiff Arms in 1955...

PAUL: Yes, you told me, Dad. (*Dials again.*)

BRENDAN: A hair-line fracture across my fore-arm and I played the last

19

twenty minutes in agony...but I stayed on and I was in plaster from here to here for five weeks after.

PAUL: Engaged. (*Dials again.*)

BRENDAN: (*Suddenly*) Bill Patterson—who also played in that game—wrote to me today, asked me to captain the golf tour to Royal Portrush in August...

SHEILA: I didn't hear that, Brendan—that's wonderful. Isn't that wonderful, Paul?

PAUL: (*Slams the phone down*) Oh, wonderful! Solves everything, doesn't it? I'll use the phone upstairs.

MARY *comes down the stairs—now dressed in jeans and a shirt.*

MARY: Oh Paul—Carmel O'Donnell saw you playing at Anglesey Road and asked me to get your autograph. She said you looked like Heathcliff the way you...

PAUL: Ah, for Christ sake, will you all get some sense! (*Goes upstairs*)

MARY: (*Calls angrily*) Well, as a matter of fact, she only said it as a joke. She said you looked stupid.

SHEILA: That's enough, Mary...

MARY: She said she wouldn't take your autograph if you wrote it in gold paint!

SHEILA: I said that's enough, Mary—I'm sure you have some studying to do.

MARY: I just want to finish this book that Aunt Catherine gave me.

SHEILA: You're finishing no book. You're studying or you're helping Michael in the kitchen.

MARY: But Mr. Rochester has just met Jane again...

SHEILA: And they'll help you get a job when you fail your exams, will they?

MARY: You weren't saying that when you had me walking around Dunnes Stores—looking like a baboon! (*Goes angrily into the kitchen*)

SHEILA: It's Catherine has her head full of that Mr. Rockerfella nonsense...

CATHERINE: (*Comes down the stairs*) Mr. Rochester! And literature is only nonsense to those who cannot appreciate its value. Ah Brendan, you are wearing your spectacles again. How much more dignified.

BRENDAN: Thank you, Catherine.

CATHERINE: Spectacles do make men so dignified—could you possibly imagine father putting those plastic things into his eyes? What are they called?

SHEILA: They are called contact lenses and they make people look younger.

CATHERINE: Do they? Well, the difference, I suppose, is that our father never needed to look younger—but I don't expect hair-dressers think that way.

Angry pause.

SHEILA: We are having dinner in the breakfast room this evening. Everyone else has agreed. (*Goes angrily into the kitchen*)

CATHERINE: The hair-dresser is rather tetchy this evening, isn't she?

BRENDAN: Her name is Sheila, she hasn't been a hairdresser for twenty-five years and...

CATHERINE: Yes, she'd like us to forget she ever was...

BRENDAN: ...and I wish to God the pair of you wouldn't go on like that.

CATHERINE: Oh, defend her—you always did. But tomorrow may open your eyes about her.

BRENDAN: Tomorrow? What's tomorrow?

CATHERINE: Your greatest failing, Brendan—as father told you time and time again—is that you never recognise a crisis until you are trapped in the middle of it.

BRENDAN: What the hell are you talking about?

CATHERINE: You see? Even now you are not aware of all the whispering, the planning, the sneaking around: your whole trouble, as father told you often, is that you take people at their face value.

SHEILA: (*Off*) Dinner, Brendan!

BRENDAN: (*Calls*) Right. (*To* CATHERINE) And your whole trouble, as father told *you* often, is that you not only read too much rubbish, but you believe it! (*Goes to kitchen*)

The hall door opens and MR. MULLIGAN *enters.*

CATHERINE: Mr. Mulligan, I've been waiting to ask you a question in this competition.

MULLIGAN: I was ringing the Angelus, Miss Ryan.

CATHERINE: I heard it and it was wonderful. (*Looks at her competition*) Now—who was the patron saint of steeple-jacks?

MULLIGAN: God, I don't know, (*Jokes*) but I heard that the patron saint of salesmen is St. Francis de Sales.

CATHERINE: (*Sternly*) Be serious, Mr. Mulligan—the prize is a 14-day tour of the Isle of Man...(*Pointed*) for two.

PAUL *comes angrily down the stairs.*

CATHERINE: Paul, do you know the patron saint of steeple-jacks?

PAUL: (*Angrily*) No—but I do know that I'm not staying in this house much longer to keep you all in the money and get treated like a shagging door-mat for my trouble. I'll shag off and leave you all without a penny and see how you get on.

CATHERINE: We would get on very well, thank you. I have my competitions...

PAUL: Going to win millions and save us all, I suppose...

CATHERINE: And Mr. Mulligan has his artificial legs.

PAUL: Has he? Well, I'm glad he's admitted to that at last. (*Goes into kitchen.*)

MULLIGAN: (*Calls*) No—I don't have artificial legs—I only sell them.

CATHERINE: That's what I meant, Mr. Mulligan. And don't you worry: I've never paid any attention to these rumours about you.

MULLIGAN: What rumours about me?

CATHERINE: Any rumour about you. Now, before we go in—are you aware of anything about to happen in this house? A conspiracy of some sort?

MULLIGAN: Conspiracy? What kind of conspiracy?

CATHERINE: I'm not certain—but I think tomorrow will tell us all. (*Takes his arm as they go into the kitchen*) Do you know that in the Isle of Man, Mr. Mulligan, the cats have no tails at all—they just have stumps. That might interest you...professionally.

MULLIGAN: (*Looks to his artificial legs in the lounge*) Yes, there could be something there...

Fade as they go in.

END OF SCENE ONE

ACT ONE

Scene Two

The following morning. Curtains are across the window. Books, magazines about the chairs. SHEILA comes briskly from the kitchen. She is dressed for the day. She takes the milk in from outside the front door, then draws the curtain. Morning light streams in. As she does this, CATHERINE—in her dressing gown—comes down the stairs. She carries a tea-pot. She goes to the toilet door. SHEILA, unnoticed, pauses to watch her.

CATHERINE: (*Turns the handle*) Good morning, Mr. Mulligan?

MULLIGAN: (*Off*) Sorry, it's engaged.

SHEILA: (*Loudly*) Good morning, Catherine—are you alright?

CATHERINE: (*Recovers*) No, I am not. Paul left me in the tea before he went off but, once again, it was cold.

SHEILA: It was hot when he left it in but, once again, you were fast asleep.

CATHERINE: I was not fast asleep—the tea was cold!

SHEILA: Alright! I'll give you a fresh pot. (*Takes it. Pause*) And by the way, there will be some changes here today that I'd like to tell you about—privately—before you go back to your room.

CATHERINE: Oh? What kind of changes?

The hall door opens and BRENDAN comes in. He has been jogging and wears colourful jogging shorts and a head-band. He wears his glasses.

BRENDAN: Ah, Sheila—what a run! What a run! Three miles flat out!

SHEILA: Lovely. Any of the others there?

BRENDAN: They were all there—Vinney, George, Sam, Tommy and a new lad called Derek whose whole business has just folded—fifty thousand up the shoot—but could he run! Off he went like a man possessed—talking to himself—none of us could catch him.

The toilet door opens and MULLIGAN comes out. He carries some surgical boots and an artificial arm-and-wrist.

SHEILA: I'll put your coffee on, Brendan. Are you off now, Mr. Mulligan?

MULLIGAN: Off to the hospital. Good morning, Mr. Ryan.

23

SHEILA *goes into the kitchen.*

BRENDAN: Good morning, Mr. Mulligan—washing a few more of your legs, were you?

MULLIGAN: No—just polishing my surgical boots this morning (*Holds up the arm-and-wrist*) and lubricating my joints. Presentation, Mr. Ryan, is the secret of sales success. (*Begins to pack his cases.*)

BRENDAN: And exercise, Mr. Mulligan. I learned that in my rugger days: out on the pitch, binding, rucking, running, tackling—all you can hear is the crowd: "Rah rah rah rah leave it to the pack/Crush them, push them/All the way back." Better than anything.

MULLIGAN: Where did I put my knee-caps? (*Picks up a box*) Here we are. Off now, I'll post your competition for you, Miss Ryan.

CATHERINE: Thank you, Mr. Mulligan—and I'll keep you informed.

MULLIGAN *goes.*

BRENDAN: (*Brightly*) All the best, Mr. Mulligan. (*Limbers up*) Well, Catherine, how are we this morning? Fighting fit, are we?

CATHERINE: If you could see yourself—a man of your age, running around the roads in his knickers.

BRENDAN: (*Determined cheerfulness*) No, that's the gear we all wear, Catherine...We all wear this.

CATHERINE: A crowd of idiots—and every one of them out of work like yourself.

BRENDAN: No no—Vinney is starting up again. And remember, father took his exercise every single morning.

CATHERINE: Father was different: he walked and he kept his trousers on while he did it. She has you dressed like an imbecile.

SHEILA *comes from the kitchen with a pot of tea.*

SHEILA: The coffee is on, Brendan—and you'd better shower and change for your interview.

BRENDAN: Right. And just coffee, Sheila. I'll catch the 9.10 Dart into Pearse. (*Runs up the stairs*) Rah rah rah rah—all the way back, all the way back...

SHEILA: Now, Catherine—your tea.

CATHERINE: Thank you—and you wish to speak to me privately about something?

SHEILA: Yes, I do—and I don't want any fuss about this. (*Pause*) I want to advise you, in advance, that there will be some work done in this house today and I'd prefer if you didn't mention it to Brendan—if *I* explained it to him *after* it had started.

CATHERINE: After what had started?

SHEILA: (*Quietly*) I intend to convert the garage into a Hairdressing

Salon. Now, with any luck, Brendan will be out at his interview when the workmen arrive—and I have no doubt that he will accept the building of the Salon once the work has begun—in the same way as he eventually accepted me taking in a lodger without me asking him to...

CATHERINE: You cannot be serious about this!

SHEILA: (*Hushed*) I am quite serious. Last Wednesday, Mr. Davis was here to assess the work and he will be back at nine o'clock this morning to begin...

CATHERINE: (*Loudly*) I really do not believe this. You want to turn that garage into a Barber's Shop?

SHEILA: A Hairdressing Salon...

CATHERINE: (*More quietly*) While your husband's back is turned?!

SHEILA: (*Pause. Controlled*) It will seat two clients and Michael will be the main hair-stylist and I will...

CATHERINE: I might have known that Michael was behind this...

SHEILA: (*Angrily*) We are not discussing Michael! I am telling you what is about to happen here today and I'm asking you to allow *me* to explain it to my husband. That is all.

CATHERINE: I see! (*Pause*) You have never changed, have you? For some strange reason, you have always seemed determined to humiliate Brendan in every way you can. First, you have him wearing those bits of plastic in his eyes, then you have him running around the streets in his underwear with a ribbon on his head and, not content with that, you now intend to turn his elegant house into a Barber's Shop. You somehow seem to have forgotten that Brendan is a top business executive...

SHEILA: *Was* a top business executive...

CATHERINE: ...and that this is a respectable area where there are standards to be maintained and codes of behaviour to be observed. People do not build Barber Shops in their gardens here—this is not Cabra, you know.

SHEILA: (*Pause. Controlled*) Can I have your assurance that you will not tell him until I...

CATHERINE: You can have my assurance that I *will* tell him—and you can have my assurance that he will certainly not allow you to build your Barber's Shop here or anywhere else.

SHEILA: (*Angrily*) Right!—and will you also tell him that while he's earning no money and too proud to get the dole that we have a mortgage, we have a bank loan, we have school fees, ESB bills, telephone bills, grocery bills—that there is a mountain of bills he won't even look at—but then maybe you can think of something better than a Hairdressing Salon to pay for all this...and maybe you'd tell *me* about it, and maybe you'd tell me about it *now*!

CATHERINE: You'd think of any excuse to change him—to reorganise his life, to turn him into your own sort...yes, and to get rid of me out of this house!

SHEILA: Oh, don't start that old thing again...

BRENDAN: (*Off*) Sheila, did you see my rugby tie anywhere?

SHEILA: (*Calls*) I left it on the bed.

CATHERINE: But I will see to it that he hears of everything before it happens and that he is allowed to take all the decisions in his own house. If you don't tell him, I certainly will.

BRENDAN: (*Off*) Sheila, I'm putting on the golf-club tie instead.

SHEILA: (*Calls*) All right. (*Pause*) Very well, Catherine—have it your way: I'll tell him *before* he goes to his interview and we'll see what he says.

CATHERINE: Good—and I will wait here to see that you do.

SHEILA: (*Sharply*) I said that I would tell him and I will tell him!

CATHERINE: Yes, very well then. (*Stands*) These conflicts you introduce into his house are both infuriating and exhausting. When I think of the girls he could have married—lovely girls at the tennis club...his own kind...dignified...

BRENDAN *comes down the stairs. Now dressed in a suit and his golf club tie. His glasses off.*

BRENDAN: I put on the golf-club tie because I might drop into Bill Patterson about the tour to Royal Portrush...

SHEILA: Oh, good idea. I'll get your coffee. (*Goes into the kitchen.*)

CATHERINE: Your wife has something to tell you before you go. For Heaven's sake, listen carefully and allow nothing to happen to your house.

BRENDAN: Don't worry, Catherine—I'm ready for anything today: jogging does that...(*Limbers up.*)

SHEILA *comes from the kitchen with the coffee.*

CATHERINE: ...And don't be an idiot all your life. (*Takes the teapot upstairs.*)

BRENDAN: Thanks, Sheila. (*Quickly drinks coffee*) After the interview, I'll get the info from Bill about the tour and also ask him if he'd like to see our photos of Barbados...

SHEILA: Brendan, would you sit down a minute...

BRENDAN: That's something we should do, Sheila—have himself and Helen over for dinner some evening—he's a good contact: five full caps for Ireland...that's a lot of influence...

SHEILA: Brendan, do you just have a minute—there's something...

BRENDAN: No, I don't Sheila—these Dart trains are all on time now...

SHEILA: But Brendan—this is very important...

BRENDAN: Then it will have to wait...

SHEILA: No, Brendan, I want to say it now...

BRENDAN: (*Laughs*) Sheila—we'll have to get you out jogging—get rid of those tensions. Now, is this eye bloodshot?

SHEILA: Brendan, would you just sit down...

BRENDAN: It's bloody sore. Anyway, I'm off. And stop worrying, Sheila—think positive.

SHEILA: Brendan...

> MARY *comes down the stairs. She is in her school uniform. She wears a Walkman and carries a crash helmet.*

BRENDAN: (*To* SHEILA) I'll phone you in the afternoon. (*To* MARY) It's getting late, Mary. (*Goes.*)

SHEILA: Brendan...

MARY: (*Sings off-key to her Walkman*) Heathcliff—it's me, Cathy come home, I'm so cold, let me in-a-your window.

SHEILA: Mary? (*Furiously*) Mary, would you stop that damn wailing...!

MARY: (*Takes off the earphones*) Sorry Mum, I didn't hear you.

SHEILA: Of course you didn't hear me with that stupid thing blaring into your ears...and fix your tie...and do you know what time it is?

MARY: It's alright—Bobby is calling for me.

> *A motor cycle is heard outside.*

MARY: There he is. (*Runs to the window*) Hi, Bobby!

SHEILA: And come home immediately after school—do you hear me?

MARY: (*Puts on her helmet*) Oh Mummy, you sound like Mother Alphonso at Assembly. (*Mimics country accent*) "I don't want any of you girls to be lounging around that Shopping Centre skitting with those punk fellows from the Christian Brothers while ye are wearing your school uniforms."

SHEILA: She's quite right, Mary.

MARY: Carmel O'Donnell said she's really telling us to take off our uniforms and then skit with them! (*Runs out*) Hi Bobby. (*To* SHEILA) A big van pulling up outside, Mum. Bye. (*She goes.*)

MICHAEL: (*Comes down the stairs*) Mummy, they're here...the van is outside...

> *The motor cycle is heard going off.*

SHEILA: I know, I know—is she gone back to her room?

MICHAEL: Yes, her door's closed.

SHEILA: Make sure.

> MICHAEL *runs upstairs. The door bell rings.* SHEILA *pauses. Then answers it.*

SHEILA: Ah, Mr. Davis—you're bright and early.

> MR. DAVIS, *a handyman, aged 60, enters. He carries a porcelain sink. His son,* BIMBO—*aged 16—carries a large roll of plastic sheeting and some tools.*

DAVIS: Oh, up with the lark, Mrs. Ryan—and we stopped off to collect one of your sinks—skipped a good breakfast to do it, but we're not complaining.

BIMBO: No, we're not complaining.

SHEILA: Oh, it's a lovely one. (*To* BIMBO) Hello.

DAVIS: That's my lad, Brian—we call him Bimbo for short. (*To* BIMBO) Mrs. Ryan that we're building the Hairdressing Saloon for.

BIMBO: How're you.

> MICHAEL *comes down the stairs.*

SHEILA: Pleased to meet you, Bimbo—and this is Michael who will be the hair-stylist in the salon.

DAVIS: (*Puts the sink down*) How do you do, sir, and may I wish you the best of luck with your new venture.

MICHAEL: Thank you very much.

SHEILA: (*Anxious to begin*) Now, Mr Davis, if you'd like to start, this is the garage...

DAVIS: (*To* MICHAEL. *Takes out cigarettes*) It won't be easy, of course—it'll take hard work and sacrifice but, as I always say, a Hairdressing Saloon is like the Undertakers, always in demand. (*Offers the cigarettes*) Do youse indulge?

SHEILA: No, thanks.

BIMBO: (*Takes one*) Thanks, Da.

SHEILA: Mr Davis, I was hoping you might begin...

DAVIS: Of course, it's all sacrifice in this recession anyway, isn't it?

BIMBO: (*Sits. Smoking*) It certainly is, Da.

DAVIS: Like us skipping a good breakfast to collect that sink: but we're not complaining.

BIMBO: No, we're not complaining—by right, I should be off teaching me mot to play snooker this morning.

DAVIS: But I said to him, "Son, this is a recession and you can leave all that until after we build this woman's saloon"—so he made the sacrifice.

BIMBO: The working classes always had to make the sacrifice. (*To* DAVIS) These smokes are very rough on an empty stomach, Da.

SHEILA: (*Angrily*) Mr. Davis! I was hoping that you might begin the work now.

DAVIS: Exactly what we're saying, Mrs. Ryan—we must be willing to

make sacrifices. Bimbo, get out my architectural plans there, will
you.

BIMBO: Right, Da. (*Searches for them in his bags.*)

DAVIS: Ever down in Dingle, Mrs. Ryan?

SHEILA: (*Coldly*) No, I wasn't.

DAVIS: They're on to me to take the caravan down there this summer but
I don't know: I hear it's so full of Japanese that you might as well
be in Peking. (*Takes the plans from* BIMBO) Now. (*Indicates the
back wall*) Your glass panel door and your panoramic window
from your waiting room into your saloon, here; your two sinks,
dryers, shelving, presses, all accessories in there, left and right;
your present garage entrance bricked up; your plumbing from
your toilet there; your toilet closed off; your water piped across
your roof; flooring, wall plastered, your paint—lights here and
here and your piped music to your waiting room and saloon, here.
How's that?

SHEILA: Yes, that seems to be everything.

DAVIS: And, as arranged, payment can be made as per our general
estimate that would include VAT, materials and labour or, if you
should prefer, payment can be made...

DAVIS/BIMBO: (*Recite together*) ...as per our special estimate that
would be paid in cash and would not require a receipt. (DAVIS
gives SHEILA *a knowing wink*)

SHEILA: What? Oh yes—cash, then. Now, I must go down to the shops,
so if there is anything you want...

DAVIS: Well, we'd only bother you for a kettle because we had to skip
the breakfast to...

SHEILA: Oh, if you'd like some coffee now, Michael can bring it out to
you.

DAVIS: Well, if it's no trouble...

MICHAEL: None whatever—would you like black or white coffee?

DAVIS: White, if you please.

BIMBO: I'll have black. And would you put a drop of milk in it?

MICHAEL: Pardon? Oh of course. (*Goes into the kitchen*)

SHEILA: And I'll see you later, Mr. Davis—and good luck with the work.
SHEILA *puts on her coat and leaves.* DAVIS *and* BIMBO *will
now begin to work: casually setting out tools and moving the
furniture to spread the plastic sheeting close to the back wall.*

BIMBO: Slow at taking hints, aren't they, Da?

DAVIS: When it suits them.

BIMBO: She didn't like you asking for cash—I could see by the way her
jaw dropped.

DAVIS: She can bounce her jaw off the floor if she likes—I wasn't going in for that credit card codology.

BIMBO: Oh the People's Revolution will put a stop to all that. (*Pause*) 'Say they've plenty of money, but. The Merc outside, rugby cups.

DAVIS: Once you hear them wanting to build saunas and gymasiums and saloons, you can be sure they have it in bucketfuls—and that they're keeping it among themselves.

BIMBO: No little backhanders for the likes of you and me—eh Da?

DAVIS: Or for anyone else. You'll find they don't exactly throw fivers at their window-cleaner or their gardener or the poor oul wan who comes in to polish around and make the tea for them. More likely pay her buttons...and by cheque at that...God help her.

BIMBO: Oh God help her is right, Da.

DAVIS: But that's not our affair—we just do our work and let them pay through the nose for it.

BIMBO: That's the way we sow the boot in, eh Da? Passive resistance...until we get the signal. Then it's power to the people and who'll carry the banner.

DAVIS: Never mind your banner and pull that sheeting right over. I'll be in the garage marking out her doors and windows. (*Goes out.*)

BIMBO *continues to spread the sheeting.* CATHERINE *comes down the stairs. She carries the teapot, a cup and saucer.*

CATHERINE: (*Angrily*) What exactly are you doing there?

BIMBO: Ah, there you are Missus; don't worry, we're putting down a bit of sheeting: you won't have much cleaning to do.

CATHERINE: I said—what are you doing?

BIMBO: We're going to build a saloon for them—in their bleedin' garage.

CATHERINE: You most certainly are not.

BIMBO: (*Laughs*) We are—honest.

CATHERINE: Has Mr. Ryan approved of that plastic sheeting?

BIMBO: I don't know what he's approved of—but we're...

CATHERINE: Where is Mrs. Ryan?

BIMBO: It's alright—she's gone down to the shops. You're game ball there. Relax.

CATHERINE: How very convenient for her.

BIMBO: Do you make the tea for them here as well?

CATHERINE: (*Controlled*) Young man, for twenty years, I made tea, breakfast, dinner, and washed, shaved and fed my father when nobody else cared two pins—and, for that, they gave me a poky room in this house and treated me like a zombie...

BIMBO: I know—and paid you buttons, by cheque. Me Da told me.

CATHERINE: I beg your pardon?

BIMBO: But don't worry: there's good times coming, roll on the Revolution, power to the class struggle, you've nothing to lose but your chains.

CATHERINE: (*Pause*) What is your name?

BIMBO: Bimbo.

CATHERINE: Good God. Are you a foreigner?

BIMBO: No—I'm from Coolock.

CATHERINE: Well, whatever you are and where-ever you are from, let me tell you that there will be no further work done here.

MICHAEL *comes from the kitchen with a tray of two coffees.*

MICHAEL: (*Guiltily*) Oh hello, Aunt Catherine.

CATHERINE: Michael, has this work been approved by your father?

MICHAEL: Been approved by my father?

CATHERINE: Don't start repeating everything like a parrot again. If he has not approved of this work—and I am quite certain he has not—then it must be stopped immediately. Is that clear?

MICHAEL: Yes, Aunt Catherine. They're having their coffee break now anyway. (*To* BIMBO) White. (*Goes out with* DAVIS' *cup*).

CATHERINE: (*To* BIMBO) You may take your time drinking that.

BIMBO: Okay. (*Pause*) Is he dead?

CATHERINE: Is who dead?

BIMBO: Your father that you made the tea for and washed and shaved and all.

CATHERINE: Of course he is dead. You don't think I left him to die alone...the way his son left him...to run off with that hairdresser.

BIMBO: No, I suppose not. (*Awkwardly*) Well, the Lord have mercy on him.

The front door opens. MR. MULLIGAN *enters.*

CATHERINE: Mr. Mulligan—I'm so glad you're here.

MULLIGAN: I had to rush back—the surgeon at the hospital wanted to see all my feet and when I went to look for them, I suddenly remembered I must have left them in a suitcase in the toilet.

BIMBO: (*Aghast*) Your feet?

MULLIGAN: But—a good prospect too: I also met an old pal who's thinking of opening a little business in Cork and he asked if I'd...

CATHERINE: Mr. Mulligan, never mind your feet and your pals in Cork—look at what is happening here.

MULLIGAN: Some decorating, is it?

CATHERINE: Some destruction. This is what the whispering was about: she has decided, without consulting anyone, to build a Barber's Shop in the garage...

31

BIMBO: It's a saloon. (*To* MULLIGAN) Did you say you put your feet...?

CATHERINE: And this is one of the persons she has employed to do it. He says his name is Bonzo.

BIMBO: Bimbo.

CATHERINE: I think we may have stopped it in time—but I will need your support until Brendan comes home.

MICHAEL *comes from outside.*

MICHAEL: Hello, Mr. Mulligan—finished your rounds already?

MULLIGAN: No, I had to rush back: I think I may have left my feet in a suitcase in the toilet.

MICHAEL: (*Casually*) I didn't notice them there. (*Goes into the kitchen.*)

BIMBO: Jaysus!

CATHERINE: (*To* MULLIGAN) If we let her away with this, heaven knows where she'll stop—next, a fish and chip shop perhaps—but, more important for us, Mr. Mulligan, we, you and I could be sent packing...

MULLIGAN: Well, at the hospital, I met this pal who's opening a butcher's shop...

CATHERINE: But what about me? (*Quietly*) I have no money, Mr. Mulligan.

MULLIGAN: Can we talk about it in a minute, Miss Ryan? (*Goes quickly into the toilet*)

DAVIS *comes from outside. He is drinking his coffee.*

CATHERINE: (*Calls to* MULLIGAN) She has no permission to do any of this. (*To* DAVIS) Don't do another thing until Mr. Ryan comes in. Michael? Michael! (*Goes into the kitchen*)

DAVIS: What's all the ructions about, son?

BIMBO: It's your woman that makes the tea for them—her father that she shaved and washed and fed for years is after dying suddenly.

DAVIS: Ah, the poor devil.

BIMBO: And she thinks we're building a fish and chip shop next and that they're going to turf her out of the house.

DAVIS: That sounds like the oul mind is going—that's called cronical shits-ophrenia.

BIMBO: But another man—I think he's a butcher—he said she wasn't to worry about it.

DAVIS: Quite right too—you see, she's not well.

BIMBO: But I don't think he's well either: he was down at the hospital and when the doctor asked to see his feet, he said he'd have to run home and get them.

DAVIS: And get what?

BIMBO: His feet. He said he left them in a suitcase in the jacks.

DAVIS: (*Disgusted*) Look, will you drink up your coffee and cut out that cod talk—we've work to do here.

BIMBO: He did, Da—honest. He's in there looking for them now.

DAVIS: (*Angrily*) And I said we've work to do here...

SHEILA *comes in. She carries some shopping bags.*

SHEILA: You got your coffee, Mr. Davis?

DAVIS: Oh, Mrs. Ryan—thanks very much—we're just looking at your lounge wall here and saying it looks very solid so I'd like to make a structural assessment for breaking in your saloon window.

CATHERINE *comes from the kitchen.*

SHEILA: (*To* DAVIS) Well, do whatever you have to do, Mr. Davis— and I'd really like you to begin as soon as possible.

CATHERINE: Not while I'm here, thank you. There will be no work done until Brendan comes home.

SHEILA: (*To* DAVIS) You may go ahead with your work now, Mr. Davis.

DAVIS: Right. Come on, Bimbo. (*They begin to strip some wallpaper from the back wall.*)

CATHERINE: You may not go ahead with anything—stop that at once, Mr. Davis. (DAVIS *stops.*) Now, did get your husband's permission to commence this work—as you promised to do?

SHEILA: Catherine, would you please go upstairs and let these men get on with what they have to do. (*To* DAVIS) Carry on, Mr. Davis. (DAVIS *continues.*)

CATHERINE: I am not going anywhere—and there will be nothing done here...stop that Mr. Davis! (DAVIS *stops.*)

SHEILA: (*To* DAVIS) Do what you were doing. (*They begin again.*)

CATHERINE: Do nothing, Mr. Davis.

DAVIS: (*Stops*) Mrs. Ryan...

SHEILA: (*Angrily*) Mr. Davis—I have told you what to do...

CATHERINE: Don't you dare do it!

DAVIS: I think she's had a bereavement in her family...

SHEILA: Mr. Davis!

DAVIS: I understand her father has dropped dead suddenly...

SHEILA: Mr. Davis, will you kindly ignore everything in this house—and do what you are being paid to do. Will you do that please?

DAVIS: (*Angrily*) Right! We're doing it! Bimbo, you heard her—ignore everything! (*They viciously tear the wallpaper*) Ignore everything.

SHEILA *goes angrily into the kitchen.*

CATHERINE: (*Following* SHEILA) Now, you listen to me—I have no intention of standing here and letting you...

33

From now, MULLIGAN *will come quietly from the toilet. He closes the door. He carries—in a carton and in his hands—a supply of artificial feet. He will sneak out and, eventually, away.*

BIMBO: (*Sees* MULLIGAN) Hey Da—look!

DAVIS: Ignore everything! (*Works on.*)

SHEILA: (*Off*) I'm not asking you to stand there—I am asking you to go up to your room—and if you really want to discuss this, we can discuss it later, in private.

CATHERINE: (*Off*) Later will be too late! Mr. Mulligan and I demand to know what is happening—and I intend to wait here until you answer me.

SHEILA *comes from kitchen.*

SHEILA: (*Back to* CATHERINE) Then wait there. (*Collects groceries.*)

CATHERINE: (*Following* SHEILA) Don't you dare run off like that! I demand to know what you told Brendan—if you told him anything. Mr. Mulligan and I are not going to tolerate what is happening here—we want that tearing stopped at once.

BIMBO: But Da...

DAVIS: (*Angrily*) Ignore everything!

SHEILA: This happens to be our house and we certainly do not need your permission to...

CATHERINE: (*Following* SHEILA) You haven't got anyone's permission—or do you think you can just rip the paper off the wall as though this were some tenement in Cabra where nobody cares what...

SHEILA: Catherine, will you please go upstairs now?

DAVIS: Sledge hammer. (*Goes out.*)

BIMBO *continues to tear off the wallpaper.* MULLIGAN *has gone.*

CATHERINE: No, I will not! I will not go anywhere! None of us will. This will be stopped. (*Knocks on the toilet door*) Mr. Mulligan?

BIMBO: He's gone, missus.

SHEILA: Then, if you won't go to your room, please be so kind as to sit down and stay quiet and let these men get on with their work. Thank you. (*Goes angrily into the kitchen.*)

CATHERINE: (*Calls*) You will not get away with this....

DAVIS *comes angrily back with a sledge hammer.*

CATHERINE: (*Calls*)...You've had too much freedom in this house... When Brendan comes home, all of this will be undone—Mr. Mulligan and I will see to it that all that wallpaper is put back exactly as it was...(*Knocks on the toilet door*) Mr. Mulligan?

BIMBO: He's gone, missus...

DAVIS: Weren't you told to ignore everything? Stand back there now...

CATHERINE: (*Opens the toilet door*) Mr. Mulligan—they're tearing off the wallpaper...

BIMBO: But Da, he's gone—he went out a minute ago with his feet under his arm.

DAVIS: Will you give up that cod talk and stand back out of my light.

DAVIS *swings the sledge hammer against the wall. A large slab of plaster falls out onto the plastic sheeting.* CATHERINE *turns, aghast to see this.*

CATHERINE: What are you doing? (*Screams*)

DAVIS *hits the back wall again. More plaster falls out, as we fade to* BLACKOUT.

ACT ONE

Scene Three

It is 5.50 p.m. same evening. A large portion of the lounge wall has been demolished, allowing us to see into the garage. There DAVIS is busily installing pipe connections. BIMBO is working in the toilet. Sinks, hair-dryers lying in the garage; door and window frames stored in the lounge. Bricks and plaster on the plastic sheeting.

MARY, dressed in jeans and sweater, sits in the lounge. She holds a crash helmet in her hand. She is quite upset with what she sees. SHEILA comes from the kitchen. She wears an apron.

SHEILA: Mary, I'm sure you have some studying to do. Mr. Davis, we're having dinner soon—could we have the water turned on again please?

DAVIS: No trouble, Mrs. Ryan, (*Calls*) Bimbo, how are you fixed for turning on your water?

BIMBO: (*Comes from the toilet*) Hey Da, there's a whole arm under the sink in there—it has fingers and all on it.

DAVIS: (*Patiently*) How are you fixed for turning on your water?

BIMBO: I'm grand, Da—but there's an artificial arm in there...

SHEILA: That belongs to Mr. Mulligan.

DAVIS: That belongs to Mr. Mulligan. Slip out and connect your water.

BIMBO: Right. (*As he goes out*) You should see it, Da. The fingers can move and all. (*Goes.*)

DAVIS: (*Calls*) And then come back here immediately and we'll finish our plumbing. (*Returns to the garage.*)

SHEILA: Thank you, Mr. Davis. (*To MARY*) Why aren't you studying, Mary?

MARY: How can I study with that in the house?

SHEILA: Very well—then you can help Michael with the dinner. Your father will be in at six.

MARY: Why didn't you tell him?

SHEILA: Now don't start that again.

MARY: When he phoned this afternoon, why didn't you tell him what you were doing?

36

SHEILA: Will you please go into the kitchen.

MARY: It's because you don't care, Mummy—Aunt Catherine is right, you don't care what the house looks like, you don't care what people think of us...

SHEILA: Will you keep your voice down. (*Sets the table.*)

MARY: Why should I keep my voice down?—everyone will know soon enough what it is. When Bobby saw it, he asked were we extending the garage for another car and I had to say yes (*Cries*) but you don't care about that, do you? You don't care that all my friends will know that my mother is washing their mothers' hair for a living! God, how will I ever face any of them again—but you don't care about that, do you? (*Runs into the kitchen.*)

SHEILA: (*Calls*) Tell Michael I need wine glasses here.

The Angelus is heard ringing as BIMBO *comes back into the garage.*

BIMBO: (*Quietly to* DAVIS) Did she say anything about the arm under the sink?

DAVIS: (*Sharply*) Look—it's none of our business if they have arms and legs and skulls and skeletons behind every inch of wallpaper in this house! We have work to do and that's that. There's six. Say your Angelus and then we'll do the roof. (*Blesses himself.*)

BIMBO: I think he's chopping them up—like Dracula.

DAVIS: Is that the way the Angelus begins? "The Angel of the Lord declared unto Mary..."

BIMBO *reluctantly blesses himself and silently says his Angelus.* MICHAEL *comes from the kitchen.*

SHEILA: (*Of the bell*) There's Mr. Mulligan ringing now—he'll be home soon too.

MICHAEL: Mummy, Mary says she's not having dinner with us.

SHEILA: Good—then let her go down to McDonalds or Wimpys and see if they'll feed her for nothing.

MICHAEL: She says the Salon will make us the laughing stock of the whole neighbourhood and if Daddy knew he'd never have...

SHEILA: (*Angrily*) Why are you telling me this, Michael?

MICHAEL: No—I'm just saying that maybe you should have mentioned it to him on the phone this afternoon so he'd...

SHEILA: He only phoned to say he'd be in at six!

MICHAEL: Sorry, Mum. (*Kindly*) No, *I* think the Salon will be great and successful and I think Dad will really get to like it once we have it open—and then it will do great business for ever and ever.

DAVIS: Amen. (*Blesses himself as he finished his Angelus.*)

BIMBO: Amen. (*Blesses himself.*)

37

The front door suddenly opens—and PAUL *comes in from work.*

SHEILA: (*Anxiously*) Oh, it's you, Paul. I thought for a minute...dinner is just ready and...and...and we have some work being done here today.

PAUL, *clearly delighted, comes silently into the lounge.*

PAUL: It's a Hairdressing Salon!

SHEILA: Yes! How did you know?

PAUL: Met Mr. Mulligan as he went squeaking down the road and he told me you were building a Salon—look at it! This is absolutely great!

MICHAEL: Do you think so?

PAUL: It's a wonderful idea.

MICHAEL: Really? (*To* SHEILA) He likes it.

PAUL: So this—once it gets going—will be the regular income for the family?

SHEILA: Yes, hopefully, Paul—Michael will be the stylist and I will just do the shampooing, combing-out, blow-drying, foaming until we see how it goes...

PAUL: It's absolutely great. (*To* MICHAEL) So you'll have a job at last.

MICHAEL: It's what I've always wanted—my very own salon.

PAUL: (*Jokes*) You'll be a wage earner for a change?

SHEILA: And we think it will take a lot of pressure off your father, too.

MICHAEL: Once he gets used to the idea...

SHEILA: And off you, Paul. You've been very good to us—but it wasn't fair holding onto you like this—and we do have Mr. Mulligan's rent as well so...

PAUL: No, no. that's okay, Mum—it was just that Judy felt we'd never get anywhere as long as I had to support... But this is great!

SHEILA: Yes. (*Laughs*) And you don't have a concert to dash off to tonight, do you?

PAUL: No, you can relax with the dinner. I'm meeting Judy at eight for drinks—but I think I'll phone her now anyway—you know women—she'll be out pricing rings when she hears this! (*Runs upstairs.*)

MICHAEL: It *will* be great, Mum—I know it will.

SHEILA: I hope so. Michael, I don't want your father bursting in on us like Paul just did—so maybe you'd go up to your room and tell me if you see him coming.

MICHAEL: Good idea. (*Runs upstairs.*)

SHEILA: (*Calls*). Mary, we need serviettes here.

DAVIS: (*To* SHEILA) We're going up on your garage roof now, Mrs. Ryan—to do your external plumbing.

SHEILA: It's gone six, Mr. Davis—if you'd like to leave that until tomorrow...

DAVIS: Well, tomorrow we'll be slipping off a bit early...

BIMBO: We have two other jobs and...

DAVIS: (*Quickly*) We have to collect materials for your dryers and your ventilators—so we'd prefer to work on now. (*Goes out.*)

SHEILA: Very well, Mr. Davis.

MICHAEL: (*Off*) Mummy, I see Mr. Mulligan's car coming.

SHEILA: Alright, Michael.

BIMBO: (*To* SHEILA) Don't forget to tell him about his arm under the sink.

SHEILA: Oh yes—I will.

BIMBO: (*Pause*) In case he's looking for it...for something. (*Waits in the garage.*)

MARY *comes from the kitchen. She throws some serviettes on the table and goes back into the kitchen.*

SHEILA: Thank you, Mary!

MR. MULLIGAN *enters.*

SHEILA: Hello, Mr. Mulligan—we heard your Angelus.

BIMBO *will now appear from the garage to listen.*

MULLIGAN: (*Goes towards that toilet*) Thanks very much, Mrs. Ryan.

SHEILA: Mr. Mulligan! I'm sorry, but that toilet will be closed off from today. We're taking the water supply for the Salon from there.

MULLIGAN: Oh. Oh, my apologies. Just force of habit.

SHEILA: But I believe one of your artificial limbs is in there...

BIMBO: It's one of your arms...with fingers on it.

SHEILA: I thought you were going onto the roof?

BIMBO: Oh yeah. I am. (*To* MULLIGAN) It's in there. (*Runs fearfully out.*)

MULLIGAN: Mrs. Ryan, I'd like to talk to you about the limbs—I don't think I'll be needing them anymore.

SHEILA: Oh? Why? What's happened?

MULLIGAN: I think my prayers may be answered and a steady job may have dropped out of the blue. A pal of mine with a butcher's shop in Cork wants me to go in with him—a full partnership.

SHEILA: (*Concerned*) Oh. And will you take it?

MULLIGAN: Well, these are hard times and it'll be a steady income and he's a trained butcher and I'm...well, apart from my unfortunate mistake with the you-know-what, I'm not exactly inexperienced ...willing to learn...

SHEILA: But you don't mean you would be moving back to Cork?

MULLIGAN: It's a great offer and I think I will, yes. Give up this game altogether.

SHEILA: You'd be leaving us?

MULLIGAN: And right away too—but I'll give you double rent, Mrs. Ryan.

SHEILA: Oh dear. I'm sorry to hear this, Mr. Mulligan.

MULLIGAN: You'll have your own business soon...

SHEILA: (*Recovers*) Yes, of course. And I am happy for you.

MULLIGAN: We can't be choosers in a recession—we have to grab whatever's going. And I bought a little bottle of champagne to celebrate... (*Takes a bottle from his pocket.*)

MICHAEL: (*Off*) Mummy! Mummy! I see him.

SHEILA: (*Calls*) Daddy?

MICHAEL: Yes—he's just stopped to chat to someone.

SHEILA: Mr. Mulligan, can we talk about this later?

MULLIGAN: Of course. And I hope your husband gets fixed up soon as well.

MICHAEL: (*Off*) They're saying goodbye now...

SHEILA: (*To* MULLIGAN) Thank you—and don't forget your arm.

MULLIGAN: (*Goes into the toilet*) I'll have to sell off all my stock now. (*Comes out carrying an artificial arm*) My partner tells me I'm to be his right-hand man. A little joke, Mrs. Ryan. (*Goes upstairs.*) CATHERINE *comes down the stairs.*

CATHERINE: Ah, Mr. Mulligan—I heard you ringing the church bell—most inspiring.

MULLIGAN: Thank you, Miss Ryan. Miss Ryan, I'd like to talk to you about...

CATHERINE: (*Quietly*) Later, I think, Mr. Mulligan—this is rather important now.

MULLIGAN: Alright—later so. (*Goes up and off.*)

CATHERINE: Now, where shall I sit?

SHEILA: Catherine, would you mind waiting in your room until dinner is ready?

CATHERINE: Yes, I would mind. I have no intention of missing this.

SHEILA: This happens to be a private matter between myself and my husband.

CATHERINE: Your husband doesn't know anything about it and you are about to get your come-uppance—and I want to see it.

MICHAEL: (*Off*) He's coming. (*Comes down the stairs*) Mummy, he's coming.

SHEILA: (*Angrily*) I heard you, Michael! Now wait upstairs please. MARY *comes from the kitchen.*

SHEILA: Mary, you wait in the kitchen.

MARY: (*Close to tears*) I want to see Daddy.

SHEILA: See him some other time. This is private.

MARY: I want to see him now. (*Sits*)

SHEILA: Right! Then Michael, you come and sit here too.

MICHAEL: I'd prefer to wait upstairs...

SHEILA: You do as you're told and wait here!

> MICHAEL *comes into the lounge and sits. Silence. The hall door opens.* BRENDAN *enters.*

BRENDAN: (*Calls*) Sheila? I'm home. Sheila, do you know that there are two men on the...(*Sees the toilet*) Good God—what's that? Sheila! Where are you?

SHEILA: In here, Brendan—we're in here.

BRENDAN: (*Comes into the lounge*) Sheila, the loo is all...(*Sees the work*) Holy Christ, what's happening here?

SHEILA: Now Brendan, this is something I was hoping to be able to tell you about in the privacy of...

BRENDAN: What's happening? What happened?

SHEILA: Brendan, don't get excited and I will try to explain exactly.

BRENDAN: The wall! The whole bloody lounge wall has been...look, the bricks are all...! Sheila, the lounge wall...

SHEILA: Yes, I know all about the wall—that is part of...

BRENDAN: And who are those men up there...? Sheila, what the hell is going on in this house?

MARY: (*Cries*) Oh Daddy...

SHEILA: Now Brendan—just calm down a minute and I'll...

BRENDAN: (*Explodes*) Will someone, for Christ's sake, please tell me what the hell is happening to my bloody house...?!

MARY: (*Incoherent and hysterical*) Oh Daddy, when I came in from school it was all broken down and our garage was being smashed in with sledge hammers and nobody cares and Bobby Collins was with me...

SHEILA: Mary, stop that at once...

MARY: Because she's doing it all for him and all he ever does is sit around here doing nothing...

MICHAEL: (*Angrily to Mary*) All you ever do is chase after Bobby Collins and fail your exams...

MARY: That's none of your business...

MICHAEL: At least *I* want to work.

MARY: You never work—you're never dragged around the supermarket...

SHEILA: Mary!

MARY: ...looking like a baboon.

MICHAEL: I often go to the supermarket!

MARY: You never do!

MICHAEL: That's a bloody lie!

MARY: It is not a bloody lie!

SHEILA: Mary!

BRENDAN: What the hell is happening here?

MARY: That Barber's Shop is happening!

MICHAEL: Will you shut-up!

MARY: No, I will not shut-up!

SHEILA: Mary, will *you* please shut-up!

MARY: (*To* SHEILA) Yes—you tell me to shut up—why don't you tell him to shut-up?

BRENDAN: (*Shouts*) Will you all bloody well shut-up for Christ sake! (*Silence*) Now, Sheila—what is this all about?

SHEILA: (*Quietly*) I had hoped, Brendan, to explain it all to you in the privacy of this room this morning or in the privacy of this room now, however...

BRENDAN: (*Quietly*) Sheila, I don't care if you had hoped to explain it to me in the privacy of the Sahara Desert—for Christ sake, just tell me what the hell is going on in my house.

SHEILA: (*Pause*) Well, as you know, we have a garage we never use and Michael is a fully-qualified Hairdresser who has not been able to get a job for the past eighteen months...

BRENDAN: Oh God, no.

SHEILA: Now Brendan, lots of people have done this—in this area too: rooms have been converted into workshops, cookery shops, keep-fit classes, beauty-parlours...

CATHERINE: (*Quietly*) It's her background...

BRENDAN: Christ...!

SHEILA: Brendan, we had all that space and it seemed perfectly obvious to use it—not only to give Michael employment, but also to provide the family with an additional income while you...well...while...while you are...eh..

BRENDAN: (*Quietly*) Go on, Sheila, say it. While I am out of work. That's it, isn't it? While I am unemployed. While I am—what is it? —unable to perform my duties as a husband and a provider. Is that it, Sheila?

SHEILA: Brendan, this is only temporary until you...

BRENDAN: And while I'm earning no money, how much do you think this "temporary" is going to cost me?

SHEILA: Brendan, when you set-up in business again...

BRENDAN: How much is it going to cost me—or have you even bothered to think of that?

SHEILA: Yes, I have—and it's not going to cost you anything.

BRENDAN: It's not? Then who's paying for it! A charity, is it? The St. Vincent de Paul? Or maybe you're holding a raffle to pay for it...

SHEILA: No, Brendan...

BRENDAN: ...or getting an EEC grant maybe. (*Angrily*) Of course I'm bloody well paying for it! Who else is there to pay for it?

SHEILA: You're not paying for it—if you must know, I'm paying for it.

BRENDAN: You're paying for it? Out of what?

SHEILA: Out of my own money, Brendan—my own savings.

CATHERINE: Oh now.

BRENDAN: (*Pause*) I see. It gets better and better, doesn't it? Out of your own savings. So you have private savings. In case I can't support the family anymore. That's a good contingency plan, Sheila. How many other contingency plans have you got?

SHEILA: Brendan, let's not quarrel about this in front of ...

BRENDAN: And when did you begin it?

SHEILA: It is only here for the time being and it is viable because the nearest Hairdresser's is four miles away in Dun Laoghaire and...

BRENDAN: (*Angrily*) When did you begin it, Sheila?

SHEILA: The work just began this morning...

BRENDAN: Yes—as soon as I had left...as soon as I turned my back...

SHEILA: (*Sharply*) Look Brendan, I'm sure you don't want to go on discussing this in front of the whole family...

BRENDAN: (*Explodes*) I'll tell you what I don't want, Sheila—I'll tell you exactly what I don't want: I don't want my wife deceiving me, humiliating me, making a fool of me in front of everyone, wrecking my house as soon as I...

SHEILA: It is not being wrecked! What I'm doing, I'm doing for your own good...

BRENDAN: It's for my own good to show up my inadequacies in front of everyone, is it! Alright. Give me the list. I'm not a good bread-winner, I'm not a good provider—am I a good husband, do I make you feel secure, am I good in bed, do I make you laugh anymore, do I look young enough with my bloody contact lenses stuck in my eyes–or have you got other plans to correct me and humiliate me?

SHEILA: How in the name of God is that Salon going to humiliate you?

BRENDAN: You don't think, do you, Sheila? It never crosses your mind what you're doing to other people.

SHEILA: What am I doing to other people?

BRENDAN: You don't even remember that you humiliated me like this before—and I said nothing about that.

SHEILA: What did I do before?

BRENDAN: You don't remember that you took in a bloody lodger without a single word to me?

SHEILA: And do you think I *wanted* to do that?

BRENDAN: And what a bloody lodger you got when you went about it— a bloody leg-less Frankenstein who came in trailing his artificial arms and legs all over the house, who invaded my privacy by sleeping in the toilets morning, noon and night—when he wasn't out ringing the church bells like the Hunchback of bloody Notre Dame.

SHEILA: And do you think I advertised for someone like that? Do you think I advertised for someone with artificial arms and legs...

CATHERINE: He hasn't got artificial legs!

BRENDAN: I don't know what you advertised for—but you couldn't have got worse if you advertised in Fosset's Circus!
Short silence.

SHEILA: Alright, I took in a lodger—but he paid good rent and God knows we needed it!

BRENDAN: Yes, that's all that matters, isn't it?—never mind if I was humiliated every minute of the day...

SHEILA: And what about me? I suppose you never did anything like that to me?

BRENDAN: Of course I didn't! I wouldn't do that to anyone!

SHEILA: So you've forgotten about her?

BRENDAN: Who?

SHEILA: (*Indicates* CATHERINE) Her!

CATHERINE: Oh now.

SHEILA: Has she become so much part of the furniture that you don't even notice her anymore?

BRENDAN: She's my bloody sister!

SHEILA: Exactly—and I have to look at her sneaking around the house and she invades my privacy and she *doesn't* pay rent...

BRENDAN: She is totally different...

SHEILA: And was I ever consulted about her coming in? No!

BRENDAN: Because she is different—she is family.

SHEILA: She is your family! Not mine!

CATHERINE: (*Furiously*) Ah now—it's out at last. I knew she always wanted to get me out of the house and now she's said it!

SHEILA: Some hope of getting you out—it would take dynamite to shift you!

CATHERINE: And you would use dynamite and bullets too because you have no class, no principles. You were a hairdresser when he found you and you're still a hairdresser.

BRENDAN: (*Loudly*) Catherine, will you shut-up!

CATHERINE: Yes, stand by her—you always did and left me to wash and shave and feed father until he died.

BRENDAN: (*Quietly*) Anyway, I want that taken down and the house put back the way it was and I want that done tomorrow. And I don't care how much it costs and I don't care if the money comes from our savings or from these private savings of yours. There'll be no hairdressing place in this house—I'm not having you going back to that—I'm not dragging the whole family back to those days. There's some dignity left somewhere.

CATHERINE: Exactly.

SHEILA: And what are we supposed to do for money! Are we supposed to go out and beg with dignity?

BRENDAN: What did we ever do for money and when did we ever have to beg! It is not staying, Sheila. It is going and that is that.

MARY: Thank you, Daddy.

MICHAEL: But, Dad, hairdressing is the only thing I ever wanted to do.

BRENDAN: I know damn well it is and I'm sick and tired listening to you talking about it for the past four years...

MICHAEL: But the Salon would be a success...

BRENDAN: ...when you should have been like Paul—out playing rugby, getting the edges knocked off yourself, having a few bones broken—and making some kind of social contacts that would get you a bloody good job.

DAVIS *and* BIMBO *come in through the garage.*

DAVIS: Excuse me, Mrs. Ryan—just to say we'll see you about nine in the morning.

BRENDAN: You'll see *me* about nine in the morning—and that is not going to be a Hairdressing Salon.

DAVIS: It isn't? You don't want a Fish and Chip shop there, do you?

BRENDAN: No, I don't want a Fish and Chip shop nor a Chinese Takeaway nor a Hamburger Joint—I want a garage there.

DAVIS: But there was a garage there.

BRENDAN: And there'll be one there again tomorrow. Just put it back the way you found it.

DAVIS: Mrs. Ryan, we have all the external plumbing in...

PAUL *comes down the stairs.*

PAUL: (*Brightly*) I phoned Judy and when I told her she...
(*Stops*) What's this—are we all queuing for haircuts already?

45

MICHAEL: There isn't going to be a Salon. It's cancelled.

PAUL: Cancelled? How can it be cancelled? It's there.

MICHAEL: It's to be all taken down—and it's to be a garage tomorrow.

DAVIS: (*To* PAUL) And the external plumbing is all done and we were going to put in the...

SHEILA: Mr. Davis, would you mind waiting outside, please?

DAVIS: (*Angrily*) Would I mind waiting outside? Oh, we don't mind waiting anywhere—just as long as you are aware that we are on time-and-a-half as from now. Come on, Bimbo.

BIMBO: (*Quietly to* CATHERINE) Weep not, sister—tomorrow belongs to the revolution.

DAVIS *and* BIMBO *go through the garage and outside.*

PAUL: Who said it's going to be a garage?

MICHAEL: Dad. He doesn't want it. Doesn't want Mum working in it and doesn't want me. Doesn't want hairdressers in the house— only rugby players...with broken bones.

SHEILA: That's enough, Michael.

PAUL: (*Angrily*) Well, let me tell you it better be a Hairdressing Salon because I'm not hanging around here supporting this family while you all...

SHEILA: Now Paul, we'll be talking to the workmen tomorrow...

BRENDAN: We're not talking to them, Sheila—we're telling them to get that bloody thing out of there—and to put the house back the way the house always was.

PAUL: But, for God's sake, why?

BRENDAN: (*Anxiously*) Because it isn't necessary, Paul—I had this very positive interview...

PAUL: Oh not again, Dad.

BRENDAN: Listen here—I had a meeting today with Bill Patterson...

PAUL: And he gave you a job, did he?

BRENDAN: Will you listen, Paul—he's already asked me to captain the golf tour to Portrush and that means business contacts, that means meeting the right kind of people, that means contact again with the old rugby crowd...

PAUL: Does it mean a job, Dad?

BRENDAN: Why do I have to explain this to everybody? Jobs aren't handed out in the middle of a recession, Paul—they come through contacts...

PAUL: Are you getting a job or not?

BRENDAN: Of course I'm getting a job—it's a matter of time, Paul...

PAUL: (*Explodes*) I knew it! I've been hearing that for the past eighteen months and meanwhile I've been bled dry financing this house, listening to you talking about interviews, listening to Judy asking me if I'm waiting until she's a dried-up old hag with her boobs hanging down to her boots...

CATHERINE: Don't be disgusting...

PAUL: Well, I'm not waiting any longer and neither is Judy.

BRENDAN: Paul, you don't understand the situation...

PAUL: I do, you want it pulled down—well, if it is pulled down, I'm leaving this house and I'm telling Judy that tonight. I'm shagging well telling her now.

SHEILA: Paul, your dinner will be ready in five minutes.

PAUL: (*Goes to get his coat*) I don't want dinner—I won't be paying for it any longer so I don't want it!

MULLIGAN *comes down the stairs. He carries his bottle of champagne.*

MULLIGAN: Hello everybody.

BRENDAN: Come in, come in, Mr. Frankenstein. No reason why you shouldn't have your say too.

MULLIGAN: I just came down to say that I'll be leaving soon. I brought a bottle of champagne to celebrate.

CATHERINE: Leaving?

PAUL: You're dead right to leave, Mr. Mulligan—get out while you can. Hop up on your wooden legs and let them fend for themselves and see how long they survive on shag all. (*Goes.*)

BRENDAN: (*Calls*) Paul, it's not as simple as...How would you feel if you worked all your life and...(*The door slams*) Ah go and bloody good riddance!

MICHAEL: (*Jumps up*) I don't want dinner either.

SHEILA: Michael, it's ready. Mary, look in at that dinner.

MICHAEL: I'm not hungry. I don't want anything here. I'm sick of this house. (*Runs upstairs.*)

SHEILA: (*Angrily*) Mary, I asked you to...

MARY: Alright! (*Gently to BRENDAN*) You were wonderful, Daddy. I knew you'd do it. You were just like Mr. Rochester. (*Goes into the kitchen.*)

MULLIGAN: Champagne. To celebrate.

BRENDAN: What are you celebrating?—have you sold another thousand knee-caps?

MULLIGAN: No, I have a real job. A partnership. And I'm moving back to Cork for it.

BRENDAN: Well, congratulations. Suddenly there are jobs everywhere for everyone.

MULLIGAN: Don't worry—you'll get fixed up—I'll keep saying the prayers for you.

BRENDAN: (*Furiously*) Don't! Don't say prayers for me, don't ring bells for me! I don't want prayers or bells—I want peace! I want a bit of respect! I want to be able to come home in the evening and see the house the same as I left it in the morning—and not in a heap of rubble. And I want that all cleared up, the wall put back and I want it done, first thing in the morning. (*Goes upstairs*) I want this house back to normal.

SHEILA: (*Calls*) Without Mr. Mulligan's rent? Without Paul's salary? Is that your idea of normal? (*Pause. To* MULLIGAN) Dinner in ten minutes, Mr. Mulligan—and we'll have your champagne then. (*Goes into the kitchen.*)

MULLIGAN: Grand. (*Pause. To* CATHERINE) Champagne to celebrate.

CATHERINE: Are you really leaving, Mr. Mulligan—or is that another rumour?

MULLIGAN: No—I'm going to be a butcher in Cork, Miss Ryan.

CATHERINE: I see. (*Coldly*) It certainly shatters the trust one puts in people—makes one wonder if the other rumours are true—and what is artificial and what is real.

MULLIGAN: Artificial?

CATHERINE: (*Goes towards the stairs*) But I daresay, I will survive. I have my competitions. Please tell Mrs. Ryan I will not be down for dinner.

MULLIGAN: But the champagne?

CATHERINE: No, thank you. I will celebrate, privately, my own achievement in maintaining the dignity of the house by having that closed down. (*Goes upstairs.*)

BIMBO *comes in through the garage.*

BIMBO: Excuse me—any idea if we're working here tomorrow or not?

MULLIGAN: I wouldn't know—I'm leaving here myself: going to spend my days sawing and cutting up meat in Cork.

BIMBO: (*Fearfully*) Oh yeah? I found one of your arms under the sink—did you get it?

MULLIGAN: Oh yes. Do you want it?

BIMBO: Do I want what?

MULLIGAN: The arm. I'm not dealing in arms anymore. A little keepsake, maybe?

BIMBO: No thanks—I have two of my own.

SHEILA *comes from the kitchen.*

SHEILA: (*To* BIMBO) Oh, I'm sorry for keeping you waiting—we'll see you in the morning at nine.

BIMBO: Me Da wants to know what will we be building in the morning?

SHEILA: You will be building a Hairdressing Salon.

BIMBO: Are you sure?

SHEILA: I am absolutely certain...and we're opening for business next week.

BIMBO: Right. (*Goes out. Calls*) We're building the Saloon, Da.

MULLIGAN *opens the bottle of champagne.* SHEILA *goes to set the table.*

THE CURTAIN FALLS.

ACT TWO

Scene One

It is one week later. The hairdressing salon has been built and is now in use. The lounge is now the waiting room with a centre table, chairs, magazines, hairdressing photos, etc. Two twin speakers high on the wall. The salon is clearly seen through a glass door and large window in the back wall with an open venetian blind. Inside, we see a fully-furnished, two sink salon with dryers, seats, towel-racks, mirrors etc. The downstairs toilet is closed off. The lounge/dining area is reduced—but retains all its previous furniture.

At the rise of curtain, MICHAEL is in the salon, cutting a customer's hair (MRS. O'SULLIVAN—aged 30). The salon door is closed. With her hair neatly styled, another customer, MISS QUINN, stands in the lounge, looking out the window, waiting. DAVIS is high on a step-ladder fixing a light. BIMBO is setting an electric cable across the hall entrance: these are last minute adjustments. The music plays softly through the speakers.

BIMBO: Hey, Da—I wish they'd put on a bit a decent music—a bit of Meatloaf or Twisted Sister.

DAVIS: You just ignore everything and get your electrics finished. We should've been out of here an hour ago.

MISS QUINN: Oh, he's coming—my boyfriend is driving up outside...

SHEILA comes from the kitchen. She carries a cup of coffee.

SHEILA: Now, Miss Quinn—some coffee while you're waiting.

MISS QUINN: Oh thank you—but my boyfriend has just arrived...

SHEILA: Oh, isn't he great...well, thank you very much for coming—and I'll give you one of our cards...

MISS QUINN: (*Takes a card*) Oh thank you—and good luck with the Salon.

DAVIS: (*Offers a card*) My card.

MISS QUINN: Thank you. (*Goes.*)

SHEILA: Thank you so much—and don't catch cold now.

DAVIS: (*Comes down the ladder*) You can leave the door open, Mrs. Ryan—we'll just check your electrics on your roof before we go.

SHEILA: Thank you, Mr. Davis. (*Goes quickly into the salon. Leaves the Salon door open.*)

50

BIMBO: (*After* SHEILA) You haven't got anything by Twisted Sister...

DAVIS: (*To* BIMBO) Will you come on and cut out that cod talk. You and your Twisted Sister.

DAVIS *and* BIMBO *carry the step-ladder outside and close the door. Now* CATHERINE *will come down the stairs. She carries some magazines and a pen. She listens—and looks surreptitiously around.*

MICHAEL: (*Expertly to* MRS. O'SULLIVAN) Now, that's looking very nice indeed. And the mousse will give it great body. You see? I've taken it right back here...collar length at the back and then just to the ears because you have that bone structure that will enhance that line... (*Combing*) Yes, lovely—and not a split end in sight, lucky you.

O'SULLIVAN: My husband used to say it was getting very thin and lanky—but then I got a great conditioner called Silkwood.

MICHAEL: Oh yes—that can work wonders—and it is certainly very strong now. So shall we dry it out and then let you see in its natural glory?

O'SULLIVAN: Thanks very much. That's lovely.

The phone rings in the lounge. CATHERINE *immediately sits into a chair in the lounge—and vigorously tosses her hair until it stands on end. She studies her competition.*

MICHAEL: (*To* SHEILA) Sheila, just dry it out, combing it right back here—and down and under here to keep that fall.

SHEILA: Okay. Grand. (*Begins to expertly blow-dry* MRS. O'SULLI-VAN's *hair.*)

MICHAEL *comes into the lounge. Now with great confidence and security.*

MICHAEL: Hello, Aunt Catherine. (*Of her tossed hair*) You wouldn't like to comb your hair if you're going to sit there, would you? (*Goes to the phone.*)

CATHERINE: I'd like you to turn off that music—I am trying to do a competition here, Michael.

MICHAEL: (*Into phone*) Good afternon—Hairstyling by Michel. (*Pause*) Today? Well, we've only opened today and we are quite busy—just let me see what I can give you... (*Looks at register*) Now, tomorrow is Sunday—day of rest—Monday, perhaps? Monday afternoon?

CATHERINE: (*Crosses to the stereo and turns off the music*) This competition is for five thousand pounds. (*Sits again.*)

MICHAEL: (*Angrily to* CATHERINE) Oh, for God's sake—don't be so stupid! (*Into phone*) No, no—not you, Madam—I wasn't referring to you at all...I was talking with my...assistant.

CATHERINE: I am nobody's assistant.

MICHAEL: (*Into phone*) Oh how nice—well, I suppose I could fit you in today if you could be with me within fifteen minutes? I have another appointment now and then I... (*Pause*) Yes, I'd be delighted to tell you about our special treatments: conditioners, colourants, setting lotions...

The door bell rings. SHEILA *comes quickly from the salon, looks at the register and turns on the music.*

CATHERINE: Excuse me—this is a competition. I need peace and quiet.

SHEILA: And this is a business and we need music. (*Looks again at the register. Memorises.*) Mrs Prendergast—a set.

MICHAEL: (*Into phone*) Just your name then and I'll put you down for twelve-forty-five.

SHEILA *opens the door to* MRS. PRENDERGAST—*late forties and very well spoken.*

SHEILA: Oh hello, Mrs. Prendergast, is it?

PRENDERGAST: Yes—I'm awfully sorry I'm late...

SHEILA: No, no, perfect time: Michel is just finished a client and he will be with you almost immediately. I'll take your coat.

PRENDERGAST: Thank you. Your advertisement was very clear but your sign is rather hidden behind that ugly tree.

SHEILA: Oh, you came from the Foxrock direction—yes, well we are hoping to put another sign in the other direction.

PRENDERGAST: Better still, get someone to chop down the tree. Most of those trees are a nuisance–they should be all chopped down. (*To* CATHERINE) Good afternoon. (*No reply.*)

SHEILA: It is just a set, isn't it, Mrs. Prendergast?

PRENDERGAST: Yes—I usually have it done every two weeks at the Bon Chance Salon in Monkstown... (*To* CATHERINE)...do you know it at all? (*No reply*) You don't? Good—I'm telling everybody to avoid it like the plague.

SHEILA: (*Awkwardly*) The Bon Chance is the one on the corner of...

PRENDERGAST: It used to be so good—but now there's Dennis who reads the *Daily Mirror* and who actually sniggered when I offered him a choice of my credit cards. I'm sure he was trained somewhere on the northside of the city.

SHEILA: I'm sure. So if you'd like to come this way...

PRENDERGAST: I think this lady is before me...

SHEILA: No, no—you can come in now.

PRENDERGAST(*To* CATHERINE) Oh you've finished, have you. (*Pause*) Yes, very nice. Suits you. (*Goes into salon.*)

MICHAEL: (*Into phone*) Thank you very much. (*Puts the phone down. To* SHEILA) Another one in fifteen minutes.

SHEILA: Did you write her in?

MICHAEL: Mrs. Brophy, yes. Is her ladyship happy?

SHEILA: I've dried her off—and she'd like to be out before one—she says her husband gets very jealous if she stays out too long. Said he'd come looking for her.

MICHAEL: God, we can't have that. (*Goes into the salon.*)

SHEILA: And Mrs. Prendergast for her set. Don't mention the Northside.

MICHAEL *closes the salon door—he can be seen attending to* MRS. O'SULLIVAN *and chatting to* MRS. PRENDERGAST. *Paul comes down the stairs. He is casually dressed and carries his rugby bag and some rugby gear. He will collect his boots and pack them.*

PAUL: I hope I can hear scissors snapping and combs combing.

SHEILA: So far—yes, you can, thank goodness.

PAUL: And Michael—has he drawn blood yet?

SHEILA: He's excellent, Paul—that's his fourth customer today and he has bookings for next week...and all from those leaflets he handed out at Dunne's Stores.

PAUL: Did Dad say anything?

SHEILA: No—nothing at all. Ignored everything. You'd think it was still a garage, the way he's going on.

PAUL: Well, as long as he doesn't try to park the car in it! (*Brightly*) Well, we have a three o'clock kick-off.

SHEILA: I left your boots inside... (*Goes to the kitchen.*)

PAUL: Thanks Mum. (*Merrily*) Hello, Aunt Catherine—I see you've gone for the Afro look.

CATHERINE: You may all be glad to know that I am not staying here. I am leaving this house for good.

PAUL: Oh? And when's that, Aunt Catherine?

CATHERINE: Quite soon. And I will be certainly glad to be away from all this stupid carry-on and to be travelling to foreign shores...with certain parties.

PAUL: Certain parties? Not to Cork with Mr. Mulligan, the squeaking butcher-boy?

CATHERINE: (*Angrily*) I know nothing of Mr. Mulligan—nor do I wish to.

PAUL: Quite right, Aunt Catherine: just think of all those people eating his meat and not suspecting a thing. Wait until they find a finger-nail on one of his sausages!

The hall door opens. BRENDAN *comes in. He has been jogging and is totally exhausted. He wears his glasses.* SHEILA *comes from the kitchen. She carries* PAUL'S *boots.*

SHEILA: Brendan, I didn't know you were out jogging.

BRENDAN: A lot you care who's out jogging.

PAUL: I'm off, Dad—we're playing Wanderers this afternoon. Bye, Mum (*Goes.*)

BRENDAN: (*Calls*) Paul, I've just run seven miles, flat out. (*The door is closed*) Oh Jesus...

SHEILA: Brendan, what have you being doing to yourself?

BRENDAN: What do you mean, what have I been doing?

SHEILA: I think you should sit down.

BRENDAN: I'm not bloody well sitting down.

SHEILA: But you're exhausted...

BRENDAN: Well, of course I'm exhausted. I've just run seven miles flat out!

SHEILA: Seven miles? You never ran seven miles.

BRENDAN: Yes, you're just like the rest of them—they all said that today too—but I ran it and I ran them into the bloody ground doing it!

SHEILA: (*Angrily*) Oh don't let me stop you! Run up the side of Dalkey quarry if you want to! Do everything—kill yourself because that's what you want to happen to you!

BRENDAN: And I suppose if you didn't even know I was out running, you couldn't be expected to know that I was also at an interview this morning.

SHEILA: This morning? Saturday morning?

BRENDAN: Yes, Saturday morning—while you and that fellow were play-acting in there with oul wans' hair, your husband was out looking for work.

SHEILA: Oh Brendan—I'm sorry—that was the Davison job, wasn't it?

BRENDAN: (*Furious*) No, it wasn't the Davison job. The Davison job was yesterday—and I know that you'll be sorry to hear that it went very well and that I wore my glasses to it and that I'm in the last eight and, if I'm successful—and I bloody well *will* be successful!— then you'll have to close down your precious Salon and let this house get back to normal!

SHEILA: Brendan, I'd be delighted if you heard that you'd got that Davison job.

BRENDAN: Good! Well, if I do hear, I'll write the news on a bit of paper and slip it under the door to you.

SHEILA: Now, Brendan, there's no need to...

BRENDAN: And while I have this privilege to talk to you—that sign that's slapped up in the front garden is a bloody disgrace (*Angrily*)...and why do we have to hear that confounded music playing all the time—or are you giving dancing lessons in here as well? *The phone rings.*

MICHAEL: (*Comes quickly from the salon*) I'll get it. (*Into phone*) Hairstyling by Michel.

BRENDAN: What did he say? What did he say into that phone?

SHEILA: It's nothing—it's only a business name.

MICHAEL: (*Into phone*) Yes, Hairstyling by Michel. Michel speaking.

CATHERINE: (*Of her competition*) How many colours in the rainbow?—seven. (*Writes it in.*)

BRENDAN: What the hell is this 'Michel' about? Who's Michel?

SHEILA: It's the name he has on the sign outside so don't try to...

BRENDAN: But not into the bloody phone! Supposing it was someone for me and he heard that!

SHEILA: It's only a trade name.

MICHAEL: (*Into phone*) I'm awfully sorry—are you for a shampoo and set?

BRENDAN: Shampoo and set! Such a bloody house to have to live in! We get rid of one circus out of the place—and in comes another: Mulligan and his Amazing Legs is hardly out the door when in comes Michel and his Amazing Shampoos.

MICHAEL: (*Into phone*) I'm so dreadfully sorry. (*To Brendan*) Dad, it's for you.

BRENDAN: (*Aghast*) What?

MICHAEL: Sorry—I thought it was a customer.

BRENDAN: And who is it for me? It's not an interview, is it?
SHEILA *quickly turns off the music.*

MICHAEL: I don't know, I...

BRENDAN: Oh, holy Christ. (*Into phone*) Brendan Ryan speaking.

MICHAEL: Sorry, Mum—I didn't realise it until...

SHEILA: I don't know how you can be so stupid!

BRENDAN: (*Forced laugh*) No, no, he's my son.

SHEILA: (*To MICHAEL*) In future, when you answer that phone, just give the number until you are certain who you are talking to.

MICHAEL: Yes, Mum. I'm sorry.

CATHERINE: (*Of her competition*) "Not a bicycle, but a one-wheeled machine usually seen in a circus". (*Pause*) A wheel-barrow. (*Writes it in.*)

BRENDAN: (*Into phone*) Yes. I see that point. I just hoped that my experience would have been a factor in...(*Pause*)

CATHERINE: Wheel-barrow won't fit. (*Crosses it out.*)
BRENDAN: (*Into phone*) Yes, of course I can collect the references from the girl at the front desk. (*Pause*) Thank you for…(*Slams the phone down. To* MICHAEL) Listen here—don't you ever lift that phone and give the name of that bloody place again.
SHEILA: I told him, Brendan.
BRENDAN: Well, it needs to be repeated because everyone seems to be bloody-well forgetting it around here.
CATHERINE: (*Of her competition*) It's a unicycle. (*Writes it in.*)
SHEILA: (*To* CATHERINE) What is!
BRENDAN: (*To* MICHAEL) And another thing—why are you suddenly calling yourself a girl's name on the phone—or has there been another development that nobody's bothered to tell me about?
MICHAEL: A girl's name?
SHEILA: It's a professional name, Brendan.
BRENDAN: It's a professional girl's name.
MICHAEL: No Dad—'Michel' is Michael in French.
BRENDAN: They why did he ask me if you were my daughter?
MICHAEL: No, Dad…
SHEILA: Brendan, lots of men change their names for business reasons.
BRENDAN: But not to girls' names! You don't hear Paul asking his rugby mates to call him Patricia, do you? There'd be a bloody stampede out of the shower if he did! (*Pause*). If you must call yourself something, for God's sake call yourself a man's name. Call yourself Jock or Harry or something.
MICHAEL: I can't say Hairstyling by Jock.
SHEILA: Attend to your customers, Michael, and don't answer back.
MICHAEL: (*Angrily*) Right! (*Goes into the salon. Closes the door.*)
    Silence.
CATHERINE: (*Reads*) "A tribe of American Indians…ending in Hawks". (*Pause*). The Tomahawks. (*Writes it in.*)
BRENDAN: (*Of* CATHERINE). Good God. (*To* SHEILA). You have this house like a bloody lunatic asylum.
    The hall door opens. DAVIS *and* BIMBO *enter.*
DAVIS: (*To* SHEILA). A final check of your electrics, Mrs. Ryan. (*To* BIMBO). Stand by, Bimbo.
BIMBO: Standing by.
    DAVIS *will now stand at the master switch and turn each light on in turn.* BIMBO *will proudly call "Check" as each lights.*
DAVIS: Sitting room/lounge! Kitchen! Dining Room Area! Hall! Vestibule! Dis-used lavatory! Scullery! And Saloon! (*To* SHEILA) And

I understand that your ball-cock and your water is now functioning to your satisfaction?

SHEILA: What? Oh yes, it's fine, thank you.

DAVIS: Good—we can pack up so, Bimbo. (*Goes out*) Excuse us butting in.

BIMBO: (*Of* CATHERINE) Da, look what they done to the oul wan.

DAVIS: Ignore everything. (*They go. The door is closed.*)

BRENDAN: I was mistaken: it isn't like a lunatic asylum. This wouldn't be tolerated in a lunatic asylum!

CATHERINE: (*Corrects*) Mohawks. (*Writes it in*) Not Tomahawks.

SHEILA: (To BRENDAN) Who was that on the phone?

BRENDAN: Oh, good news as far as you're concerned: Davisons said they wanted someone younger and told me to bugger off. (*Angrily*) But, by God, I'll surprise you all yet—I'll land a job that will take you all by surprise.

SHEILA: I'll run your bath for you. (*Goes upstairs.*)

BRENDAN: Oh sorry—in the way down here too, am I? Well, don't worry—I'll be out at another interview on Monday.

CATHERINE: (*To* BRENDAN. *Quietly*) Of course, you only have yourself to blame for this. Next, you'll have to ask her for money to buy a newspaper.

BRENDAN: What happened to your hair?

CATHERINE: Nothing happened to my hair.

BRENDAN: It looks as though you had a thousand volts of electricity shot through it.

CATHERINE: Well you won't have to look at it much longer because I'm leaving this house.

BRENDAN: Leaving? How can you be leaving? Where can you go?

CATHERINE: Arrangements are being made with certain parties.

BRENDAN: You don't mean Mulligan, do you?

CATHERINE: (*Furiously*) Why does everybody associate me with that man? I know nothing about him nor do I want to. For all I care, he can stay in Cork and sell his sausages—with finger-nails or without finger-nails on them.

BRENDAN: Finger-nails on what?

MICHAEL *comes from the salon with* MRS. O' SULLIVAN. *He switches on the music.*

MICHAEL: (*Very confidently*) Now, Mrs. O'Sullivan, I'd like to see you again in, say, four weeks for a slight re-styling—and I think that you'll find that if you sweep it back at the sides, you'll get that lovely gentle fall in front.

O'SULLIVAN: Thanks very much, Michel. Here. (*Gives him a twenty pound note*) And I'd better hurry before my husband thinks I'm out too long.

MICHAEL: Nothing smaller? Our first day and we're a little short of change...

O'SULLIVAN: No—my husband only had large notes...

MICHAEL: Never mind. I'll get change upstairs. (*Goes quickly upstairs.*) *Silence.*

O'SULLIVAN: They have it very nice, haven't they? (*Silence*) I wonder what it was before it was a Hairdresser's.

BRENDAN: It was a home.

O'SULLIVAN: Was it really? (*Looks from* CATHERINE *to* BRENDAN) A home for what?

BRENDAN: A home for people to live in, a home where a man could talk to his family in, a home to see your wife in occasionally—and not to have people galloping through it as if it were a public lavatory in O'Connell Street.

O'SULLIVAN: Oh, that kind of a home? (*Pause*) I hear they're putting another sign outside—So Michel told me.

BRENDAN: Did he? Amazing how you hear these things, isn't it?

O'SULLIVAN: Yes. (*Pause*) Are you here to collect your wife?

BRENDAN: Collect my wife? Yes, look at me: I was out jogging and I suddenly thought to myself: I know what I'll do: I'll run over and give her a piggy-back across to the house!

MICHAEL: (*Comes down the stairs*) Now, here we are. (*Gives* MRS. O'SULLIVAN *her change*) And I'll see you in about four weeks. (*Takes out a card*) And one of my cards so you won't forget me.

O'SULLIVAN: Oh, I won't. And if my husband calls will you tell him I'm gone. (*Goes*)
The phone rings in the lounge.

MICHAEL: I certainly will. (*Closes the door*) Alright—I'll get that...

BRENDAN: (*Angrily*) Don't touch that phone! (*Goes to the phone. To* MICHAEL) Do you think I could have this *without* the musical accompaniment?

MICHAEL: Pardon? Oh yes. Sorry, Dad. (*Turns off the music.*)

BRENDAN: Thank you. (*Into phone*). Brendan Ryan speaking. (*Pause*). Oh hello, Bill...(*Now with sudden enthusiasm*)...you know, Sheila and I were just chatting about yourself and Helen going to Barbados and she was saying that we also have some home movies you should see...(*Pause*). Yes. I suppose we can expect Portrush to be a bit cooler. (*Pause. Laughs*). Oh, you heard about that, did

58

you?—it's being run by my son, Michel (*Corrects*) Michael! and...(*Pause*). You don't want me to put your name down for a short back-and-sides, do you? (*Laughs. Then*) Well, Bill, I'd certainly like to hear about that—and thanks very much for keeping me in mind—very decent of you. (*Pause*). Look, Bill, let me take this upstairs—someone's playing the stereo down here. (*To Michael*). Put that down when I get him upstairs. That's Bill Patterson.

MICHAEL: Alright, Dad.

SHEILA: (*Comes down the stairs*) Brendan, your bath is ready.

BRENDAN: (*Anxiously*) That's Bill Patterson on the phone and he wants to talk to me urgently—he said something has come up that might interest me.

SHEILA: You mean a job?

BRENDAN: (*Panic*) I think so. I don't know. I don't know whether it is or not. It mightn't be anything at all. (*Runs upstairs.*)

CATHERINE: (*Of her competition*) "Legendary creature who flew into the sun and then fell to earth". (*Pause*) Superman. (*Writes it in.*)

SHEILA: (*To* MICHAEL) What about Mrs. Prendergast?

MICHAEL: She wanted to look at the catalogue of hair-styles before I did anything.

SHEILA: She must have it off by heart by now.

> MICHAEL *and* SHEILA *go into the salon, close the door and can be seen attending to Mrs. Prendergast.*

CATHERINE: (*Correcting*) Superman won't fit. (*Pause*) Oh, that legendary horsy thing that could fly...

> *A motor-cycle is heard outside. The hall door opens and* MARY *comes angrily in. She is dressed in motor-cycle leather, but without her crash-helmet. The motor-cycle is heard going off.*

MARY: I hope you hit a brick wall! (*Slams the door*) I hope the petrol tank explodes under you and blows your (*Sees* CATHERINE)...your goggles all over the road.

CATHERINE: Mary, what was that thing that flew into the sun?

MARY: I didn't see anything flying into the sun.

CATHERINE: Oh now—you haven't had a tiff with your Mr. Bobby Collins, I hope?

MARY: Don't mention his name. It's all off—for good! (*Cries*) And do you know why?—because of that! Once he saw what that was, I could see he was getting more ashamed of me by the minute.

CATHERINE: Oh dear...

MARY: God, what will everyone say now? They'll all know why he left me. Oh, Aunt Catherine, I wish I was like you—you sit here and just read and watch us all making fools of ourselves.

CATHERINE: Yes—but not for much longer, Mary. I am leaving this house.

MARY: Where are you going?

CATHERINE: To foreign shores, most likely. Arrangements are being made with certain parties and as soon as I get the results...

MARY: (*Excited*) Oh, Aunt Catherine—have you heard from Mr. Mulligan?

CATHERINE: (*Angrily*) I have not heard from Mr. Mulligan—nor do I wish to! There is more to life, Mary, than a Cork butcher whose legs are even open to question—not to mention his sausages!

MARY: That's what I should have said to Bobby Collins when he snapped back his crash-helmet: (*Haughtily*) "I am sorry—you will not see me again because I am travelling to foreign shores with certain parties." Oh, that would have really fixed him.

The door-bell rings. SHEILA *comes quickly from the salon.*

SHEILA: Oh hello, Mary—I didn't hear you come in. Have you been crying?

MARY: (*Angrily*) Why would I be crying?

SHEILA: (*Looks at the register*) Then you should ask Bobby Collins to get you goggles for that motor-bike—your eyes are very red. (*Memorises*) Mrs. Brophy—cut and blow-dry.

MARY: (*Cries*) Well you needn't worry about them because I won't be here much longer. I'm going away to foreign shores. (*Runs into the kitchen.*)

SHEILA: (*To* CATHERINE) Doing the same competition, is she? (*Goes to the door.*)

CATHERINE: (*Of her competition*) That's right—he had wings on his back...

SHEILA *opens the door to* MRS. BROPHY—*aged 45, too well dressed with a very striking hair-style. A very inquisitive woman.*

SHEILA: Oh hello; Mrs. Brophy, is it?

BROPHY: That is correct, yes. (*Look curiously around.*)

SHEILA: Please come in. You phoned earlier this morning.

BROPHY: That is correct, yes.

SHEILA: Michel is with a client at present—but if you like to take off your coat, I can bring you directly into the Salon.

BROPHY: Oh grand, yes. (*Takes of her coat.*)

SHEILA: You didn't have any trouble finding us, did you?

BROPHY: No, I didn't—but I was here before.

SHEILA: (*Hangs her coat*) We're considering a new sign outside to...
(*Stops*) You were here before?

BROPHY: I was, yes. The breakfast room is out there, isn't it?

SHEILA: But we only opened today.

BROPHY: Ah no—not to have my hair done. No, with my husband,
Danny—he was starting out in the electrical business at the time.
You're from Cabra, originally, aren't you?

SHEILA: Pardon? Yes.

BROPHY: Same as myself, yes. No, you probably wouldn't remember us,
but your husband gave a big do here for all the sub-agents and
Danny was one of them. He has his own business now.

SHEILA: And you are living here...?

BROPHY: 'Deed we're not. Still in Cabra (*Laughs*) but Danny says
always do your shopping where the hungry rich go—they know
how to stretch a penny. Driving up in their Mercedes, and then
killing one another for the special bargains.

SHEILA: (*Coldly*) Yes. So, you'd like a cut and blow-dry...?

BROPHY: Well, now that I'm here, I might make the evening of it and
have a perm.

SHEILA: (*Angrily*) A perm.

BROPHY: Tell us—was it very expensive to have all this done?

SHEILA: Not too expensive—now if you'd like to come inside?

BROPHY: I think this lady is first. (*Indicates* CATHERINE)

SHEILA: No, she's not. She's just my sister-in-law.

CATHERINE: (*Suddenly, of the competition*) "Pegasus" is the name!
(*Writes it in.*)

BROPHY: Pleased to meet you. Eileen Brophy is my name.

BRENDAN: (*Off*) Sheila? Sheila?

SHEILA: This way if you please, Mrs. Brophy.

BROPHY: (*Indicates*) They should have covered in those cables.
BRENDAN *comes quickly down the stairs. He only wears his
jogging shorts.*

BRENDAN: (*Excited*) Sheila, Bill Patterson said he... (*Sees* BROPHY)
Oh blast it...!

BROPHY:And you have a sauna upstairs, do you?

SHEILA: No, this is my husband—he has been out jogging.

BROPHY: Oh yes, I remember him. (*Quietly to* SHEILA) Gone very
grey. Have you no Grecian 2000?

SHEILA: I think Michel is ready for you now, Mrs. Brophy.

BROPHY: Oh grand, yes. (*To* CATHERINE) I'll see you later, Mrs.
Pegasus. (*Goes into the salon.*)

SHEILA: This is Mrs. Brophy, Michel.

MICHAEL: (*To* BROPHY) Oh hello.

SHEILA *closes the venetian blinds and comes out.*

SHEILA: Sorry, Brendan.

BRENDAN: (*Angrily*) How long is she going to be here?

SHEILA: She said she wants a perm—could be four hours.

BRENDAN: Oh holy Christ!

SHEILA: She'll be in there and she's the last for today. What did Bill Patterson say?

BRENDAN: Bill Patterson said he's coming here—and look what I have to bring him into!

SHEILA: He's coming here?

BRENDAN: Yes, here—to this shambles of a house.

SHEILA: When, Brendan?

BRENDAN: At half-five before he flies out to Paris for talks about opening a new European Agency there.

SHEILA: A European Agency? And he wants to come over and talk to you about it first?

BRENDAN: (*Angrily*) Well, I hardly think he wants to come over to get a hair-cut. Yes, he wants to talk to me about it...or something—he said it was a business proposition that he...Christ, Sheila, of all the days you picked to open up that bloody monstrosity.

SHEILA: Now, Brendan, no-one knew Bill Patterson was coming over to give you a business proposition today...

BRENDAN: He didn't say he was *giving* me a business proposition!

SHEILA: Well, whatever he said—you can both have drinks here, no-one will disturb you, we can take all the phone calls upstairs...

BRENDAN: And what if that bloody golly-wog walks out just as he's making me some offer?

SHEILA: She won't—I'll tell Michael to keep her in there and Catherine will stay in her room and I'll tidy up here and you can discuss your business in total peace.

BRENDAN: (*Goes upstairs*) Total peace?—it'll be like trying to do a business deal in the middle of a three-ring circus. (*Goes off.*)

SHEILA: It will be fine, Brendan. And I'm glad. I really am glad, Brendan. And your contact lenses are in the bathroom.

The hall door opens. DAVIS *and* BIMBO *look in.*

DAVIS: We're off now, Mrs. Ryan...if you'd like to fix up with us.

SHEILA: Oh yes—I'll get my handbag. (*Goes into kitchen*).

DAVIS: (*Calls*) In cash!

BIMBO: Hey Da, look—the oul wan is gone all punk.

DAVIS: I told you to ignore everything.

CATHERINE: (*Suddenly*) I have it. It wasn't a legendary *horse* that flew
    away—it was Icarus. (*Writes it in.*)
BIMBO: (*To* CATHERINE) No, it *was* a horse—(*laughs*) it was Shergar!
DAVIS: *(Pulls* BIMBO *away)* What did I tell you!
CATHERINE *stops to count the letters...As the* CURTAIN FALLS.

ACT TWO

Scene Two

It is five-thirty, same day. The venetian blinds are open again in the salon and we can see MRS. BROPHY *sitting under a hood dryer, reading a magazine. In the lounge,* MARY *is on the phone. She now wears jeans and sweater.* SHEILA *now comes down the stairs, carrying* BRENDAN'S *golf clubs which she will place conspicuously. Throughout the following, she will also rearrange the rugby photos and trophies and take some glasses and bottles from the drinks cabinet.*

MARY: (*Into the phone sweetly*) Hello, Bobby. It's me. I'm just ringing to tell you that I think I left my scarf—the blue one—inside your crash-helmet...(*Pause. Now sharply*) Alright, if it isn't there, it's somewhere else—but what I'm ringing to say is if you do find it, I don't want it back because I won't be here: I expect to be travelling abroad quite soon to foreign shores. Arrangements are being made with certain parties and now I'm so sorry, I cannot discuss this with you any further: I'm expecting certain parties over this evening. Good-bye. (*Slams the phone down.*)

SHEILA: Mary, your father will want to speak privately with Bill Patterson in the lounge, so don't sit around.

MARY: Michael says don't use the phone, you say don't sit around, Bobby says don't get on his bike—what do you all want me to do...drop dead?

BRENDAN, without his glasses, comes down the stairs. He is dressed in dark slacks and a shirt.

BRENDAN: (*Testily*) Sheila, have you seen my golf-club tie anywhere?

SHEILA: I think it's hanging with your club blazer—but do you think you ought to wear it?

MARY: It's all off between me and Bobby, Dad.

BRENDAN: In a minute, Mary. (*To Sheila*) Why shouldn't I wear it? If I'm wearing it, at least he'll know I have an interest in the golf.

SHEILA: But I don't think you'd be wearing a golf-club tie on a Saturday afternoon—it might be better to be casual. And anyway, I've left your golf-clubs here so he can see them.

64

BRENDAN: And supposing *he's* wearing his golf-club tie!

MARY: Dad?

SHEILA: I doubt if he will, Brendan.

BRENDAN: But if he is, he'll wonder why I'm not.

SHEILA: I really think a sweater and your grey trousers would be more appropriate for a Saturday.

BRENDAN: (*Angrily*) Christ! Change again—this is the fourth pair of trousers I've put on. Is that scare-crow still in there?

SHEILA: I'll have Michael close those blinds so she can't see out.

BRENDAN: (*Goes upstairs*) And lock the door so she can't get out!

MARY: Dad—did you hear about Bobby Collins and me?

BRENDAN: (*Absently*) Yes, Mary, that's grand—just be careful on that motor-bike of his and always wear that crash-helmet he gave you.

MARY: (*Angrily*) I don't have his crash-helmet, Dad, because he said I...

BRENDAN: (*Angrily*) Then, Mary, get one of your own—I'm not having you going around on a motor-bike without a crash-helmet and that's that! (*Goes upstairs*) Grey trousers.

MARY: (*Angrily*) That's what's wrong with this house—nobody gives a damn about anyone. The only person I can talk to has decided to leave for foreign shores...

PAUL *has come in the front door. He carries his football gear—and has a plaster on his forehead and a black eye.*

PAUL: (*Brightly*) I'm not leaving yet, Mary—you can talk to me.

MARY: You! All you can talk about is your rugby and the bank and Judy and I'm delighted they gave you a black eye. (*Runs crying into the kitchen.*)

SHEILA: Paul—that looks dreadful—let me see it...

PAUL: It's all right—we beat them. (*Of* MARY) What's wrong with her?

SHEILA: You'd better let me put something on it. What happened?

PAUL: It's alright—it was just a high tackle. What about Mary?

SHEILA: It's all over between herself and Bobby Collins.

PAUL: Oh—Heathcliff on wheels.

SHEILA: Did the doctor see that eye?

PAUL: Yes, yes. How's the Salon going?

SHEILA: Oh very good—but even bigger news. (*Quietly*) Bill Patterson phoned to say he's on his way to Paris to open a Marketing Agency and he's calling to see your father before he goes!

PAUL: When?

SHEILA: He should be here now.

PAUL: About a job? He has a job for him.

SHEILA: Yes—Brendan is afraid to even admit it to himself—he's been running around like a ferret for the past hour...But when Bill comes, would you take all the phone calls upstairs...and the Register...

PAUL: Oh Mum, it could all be beginning to happen, couldn't it? Mulligan gone, Michael in the Salon, Dad getting a marketing job again...

SHEILA: Paul, after the last eighteen months, I can hardly believe it.
The door bell rings.

SHEILA: God, there he is.

PAUL: (*Takes the register*) I'll go upstairs.

SHEILA: (*Excitedly*) No. Stay here a minute. He likes you. Chat to him about rugby for a while and make sure Mary doesn't come bawling out of that kitchen...and keep Aunt Catherine upstairs when you go there...
The door bell rings again.

MICHAEL: (*Comes smartly from the salon. Turns on the music*) I'll get it.

SHEILA: Will you turn that off and get back into the Salon and draw those blinds and don't let that woman out even if she puts a gun to your head.

MICHAEL: Right. Sorry, Mum. (*Turns off the music and goes back into the salon, where he will close the venetian blinds.*)

SHEILA: (*Loud whisper*) Brendan? Brendan, can you hear me?

BRENDAN: (*Off*) Where did you leave my blue sweater?

SHEILA: Put on the grey one. Brendan, that's him at the door now.

BRENDAN: (*Angrily, off*) And what are you doing? Waiting for him to climb in through the bloody window? Let him in!

SHEILA: Are you alright there, Paul?

PAUL: Yes Mum—let him in!
The door bell rings again as SHEILA *opens the door to* BILL PATTERSON—*a very assured and elegant man of 50, wearing glasses, dressed in a suit and golf-club tie.*

SHEILA: Bill, how lovely to see you again.

BILL: Sheila—beautiful as ever.

SHEILA: Helen isn't with you?

BILL: No—I'm actually on my way to the airport—so this is really just a dash in and out. (*Checks his watch.*)

SHEILA: Oh, what a pity—we must arrange to have you both over some evening. (*Of* PAUL) Look at this one—home from the wars.

BILL: Paul. (*Shakes hands*) Now that is a shiner to be proud of. A real beauty, that one.

PAUL: A high tackle in the last minute, Mr. Patterson.

BILL: But worth it. Gerry O'Dowd was at the game: said you played splendidly. And didn't I see something about you in the *Times* last week?

PAUL: That was on Wednesday...

SHEILA: Bill, we still have some of our Caribbean photos and I've selected a few reels of film that you and Helen can...

BILL: Lovely idea and I must get them from you sometime—but I really have to dash to this Paris meeting: a new European Agency in the offing and I thought I'd just squeeze in a quick word with Brendan first.

SHEILA: Oh wonderful. I'm sure he'd like to hear whatever you have to say. I'll call him: he's busily preparing a financial report for some new German company. Paul, a drink for Bill, please. (*Goes upstairs*)

BILL: Small whiskey would be fine, Paul.

SHEILA: (*Off*) Brendan? Bill Patterson is here to see you.

BILL: (*To Paul*) I suppose you know that earlier in the season, your name was mentioned for an International trial?

PAUL: They're always saying that, Mr. Patterson—never happens though..

BILL: Well—keep this strictly among ourselves—I heard something a lot more definite for next season...if you keep your form.

PAUL: That would be great, Mr. Patterson. I keep remembering that you had five full caps when you were my age.

BILL: (*Takes the drink*) A lot of luck, Paul, and a lot of determination: and being in the right place with the right people at the right time. It often comes down to that in the final analysis. Contacts. Well worth remembering.

BRENDAN *and* SHEILA *come down the stairs.* BRENDAN *wears a blue sweater.*

BRENDAN: Bill! sorry to have kept you waiting....

BILL: Not at all, Brendan...

BRENDAN: Just doing a bit of painting in the bathroom...

SHEILA: (*Quickly*) And preparing that financial report for the Germans, darling.

BRENDAN: The Germans? Oh yes—I was at that too...

BILL: Well, hopefully, we may soon be able to get you to work for the Irish.

BRENDAN: Oh yes?

BILL: And I was telling Paul that I heard on the grapevine that he could have a Trial next season.

BRENDAN: Oh excellent. We have high hopes there. You have a drink, Bill...?

BILL: Yes, yes—and just this and I'm off. (*Checks watch.*)

BRENDAN: I'll have that too then. Sheila?

SHEILA: I'll have a G and T.

BILL: (*To* BRENDAN) Well...I was really hoping for a little man-to-man chat...

SHEILA: (*Sweetly*) Oh, then I'll sit here and stay nice and quiet.

BRENDAN: (*Brightly*) Good. (*Gets the drinks.*)

PAUL: I'll see you later, Mr. Patterson.

BILL: Very good, Paul. Keep up the form, hit them low and hit them hard and don't forget the old chant: Rah rah rah rah / Leave it to the pack / Push them, Crush them...

BRENDAN/BILL/PAUL: ..."All the Way Back."

PAUL: (*To* SHEILA) I'm taking the book, Mum. (*Goes upstairs.*) *Awkward silence.*

BRENDAN: Well—cheers everybody.

BILL: Yes, indeed—cheers. *They drink. Short silence.*

BILL: You don't wear the glasses anymore, Brendan.

BRENDAN: What? No, no, don't really need them. (*Pause*) You're wearing the golf-club tie, I see, Bill.

BILL: Oh yes. Like to wear it as much as possible.

BRENDAN: Yes, so do I—but not with a sweater, of course.

BILL: No. (*Laughs*) Or with the pyjamas—as they used to say.

BRENDAN: (*Laughs*) Yes—what was it Butty Wilson used to tell us after training?

BILL: Oh yes...

BRENDAN: "I want you to wear your club scarves at all times—even if you're only wearing your pyjamas or your jock-strap".

BILL: Yes. That's it. (*Laughs. Pause*) And Catherine?

BRENDAN: (*Laughs*) Oh yes—she always wears her scarf with her jock-strap.

BILL: (*Mock horror*) Sheila, how do you put up with this fellow?

SHEILA: You get used to it, Bill.

BRENDAN: Seriously, Bill—Catherine was never better.

BILL: Good. A woman of great style and dignity. Helen is terribly fond of her.

BRENDAN: We all are, Bill, we all are. *Awkward silence.* BILL *looks at his watch.*

BILL: To business then?

BRENDAN: Yes.

BILL: Right. Now, I really considered this call quite necessary *before* the weekend because of a series of developments that have suddenly

68

arisen...which I feel you should know about and could be very much to your benefit.

BRENDAN: Well, thank you very much, Bill.

BILL: Now, in outlining these, I must wear—from time to time—a few of my hats: three different hats, in fact—and my first hat is my Businessman's Hat. And here, Brendan, I must tell you that I was having dinner with Gerry O'Dowd last week—this in the strictest confidence, mind you...

BRENDAN: Of course, Bill, of course...

BILL: ...and he mentioned that he had an application from you for a marketing position with one of his companies.

BRENDAN: Oh?

BILL: Probably Travels International Enterprises—T.I.E.—would that be the one?

BRENDAN: T.I.E.? Oh yes—I think, just out of interest, I may have fired in an application...but I didn't know that Gerry owned T.I.E.

BILL: Yes, that's one of his—but what he said was that he was delighted to get your application—delighted and quite excited about it and I, naturally, said so he should be: didn't he know as well as I that Brendan Ryan had an excellent track-record on the international rugby pitch as well as in the international business world.

BRENDAN: Well, that was very decent of you to say that, Bill.

SHEILA: Indeed it was...

BILL: And I think it will carry some weight. He tells me he has one hundred and fifty applications for the job so far—but don't let that discourage you here, Brendan: I happen to be a great believer in the maxim that the right word at the right time can always do the trick—it can, in the dying seconds of any game, let a man in around the blind side, send him darting along the touch-line, jigging through the defence, selling the dummy and in at the corner flag, so to speak.

BRENDAN: Well, I must say I very much appreciate that, Bill.

SHEILA: Yes, you really are very good, Bill.

BILL: Not at all. (*Looks at his watch*) Which brings me quickly to hat number two—and I hope now you will take this in the spirit it is intended and not be, in any way, offended by what I have to say.

SHEILA: Of course not, Bill.

BRENDAN: I think we know each other well enough, Bill—on and off the pitch.

BILL: Good. Well, hat number two is my hat as a member of the Residents Association and, in this regard, I think it is only fair to mention—in passing—that there are certain murmurings in the

Association about—what shall I say?—about a recent building development here. There has been quite a vocal reaction to it at one of our recent meetings...

SHEILA: (*Laughs*) You don't mean our Hairdressing Salon, do you?

BILL: Yes, Sheila, unfortunately I do mean it—and I'm desperately sorry to have to bring this up at all...

BRENDAN: No, no, Bill—that's all right...

BILL: There are just general questions about...oh, suitability of having it sited here, the general decline in the valuation of property in the area...that sort of thing. General disquiet, so to speak.

BRENDAN: I see. And what exactly is being suggested, Bill?

BILL: Well, I don't think they are suggesting anything...but, if I were asked, I'd say a rather obvious solution—in the light of these objections—would be to discontinue it. To close it.

SHEILA: But why?

BILL: (*Slightly annoyed. Sweetly*) Why? For the reasons I have given, Sheila—the residents' objections.

SHEILA: And because they object, you say we should close it?

BILL: Now, I didn't say that. I am merely informing you—in passing—of the objections...

SHEILA: But whose objections?

BILL: The residents' objections.

SHEILA: But which ones? Which resident?

BILL: Well, Sheila, objectors are usually reluctant to display their names in lights...

SHEILA: Well, I haven't heard any—in lights or otherwise.

BILL: That doesn't mean there haven't been any.

SHEILA: Our next-door-neighbours certainly aren't objecting.

BILL: Well, others apparently are.

SHEILA: The one on this side has actually made an appointment for a shampoo and set and...

BILL: Which is totally immaterial, Sheila—the fact is that there have been objections...

SHEILA: How many have there been?

BILL: (*Testily*) I don't know how many there have been!

SHEILA: Has there been ten, twenty, more than twenty, thirty, more than thirty, forty—

BILL: (*Loudly*) Now look here, I'm not going to be drawn into this. I am telling you there are objections and that's that. (*Stops. Calmly*) I'm sorry, Sheila—but that is the situation. And I do have a flight to catch.

BRENDAN: Yes, of course, Bill—and we shouldn't delay you any further. We really do appreciate, most sincerely, what you said on my behalf to Gerry O'Dowd and also what you said for Paul—and don't worry about the Salon: we'll have a little chat here between ourselves and I'm sure we can come to some arrangement.

BILL: (*Sharply*) Good. And I'd like you to have that little chat between yourselves and come to some arangement *over this weekend*—because I'll be seeing Gerry on Monday and it would be of benefit to know your decision by then.

BRENDAN: (*Puzzled*) You mean our decision about the Hairdressing Salon?

BILL: Yes—I mean your decision about the Hairdressing Salon!

BRENDAN: (*Lightly*) But what has Gerry to do with whether we decide to open the Salon or...

BILL: (*Looks at his watch*) I don't think you are listening, Brendan.

BRENDAN: I think I am, but I don't...

BILL: Then you clearly don't understand what you're listening to!

BRENDAN: No, Bill—I simply don't see what it has to do...

BILL: Then let me put it this way: if I were interviewing you for a marketing job, it would certainly have a lot to do with me.

BRENDAN: But why?—if this is a private...

BILL: (*Angrily*) Good God, Brendan! All right—basics! What does marketing mean? It means entertaining clients, in the convivial atmosphere of one's home—and, with the greatest respect, I don't see much evidence of a convivial atmosphere in this house to entertain prospective clients or any other kind of clients. (*Sweetly*) I'm sorry, Sheila...

SHEILA: Are you saying, Bill, that Brendan couldn't entertain clients here because of...

BRENDAN: (*Nervously*) Now, Sheila....

BILL: I am saying that it is not suitable—this house is not suitable to entertain anyone and that is the sum total of it and I must apologize if that is being too blunt but there you are!

SHEILA: But how is it not suitable?

BILL: It's not a question of how—it simply is.

SHEILA: It simply isn't, Bill—we have always entertained people here...

BILL: Yes—in the past.

SHEILA: There is no difference now.

BILL: Well, of course, there's a difference.

SHEILA: There isn't—that Salon closes at six o'clock...

BILL: That isn't the point. (*Looks at his watch.*)

SHEILA: It *is* the point—after six, this house is just like any other house...

BILL: (*Angrily*) It is not like any other house and you'd be a fool to think it is...

SHEILA: After six, Bill, this house is just like your house.

BILL: It is most certainly not like my house!

SHEILA: It is, Bill—that Salon closes up and there...

BILL: (*Furiously*) Oh for God's sake, let's not fool ourselves about this any longer: before or after six, this house is not like my house or any other house in this neighbourhood—it has a vulgar hoarding outside, it has been turned into a Hairdresser's, it will have customers walking in and out all day—and all of this has been done in the most cavalier and selfish fashion without a single word of consultation with me or with anyone and, I assure you, that it is not going to be tolerated by any of us.

SHEILA: By any of who?

BILL: By any of us. By the residents. (*Loudly*) Alright, Sheila, by me. By my wife. The entire valuation of this area is now at risk—and that will certainly not be tolerated. Your Salon will be closed-up and I can tell you now that if it isn't...(*Stops*)

SHEILA: Yes, if it isn't?

BILL: If it isn't then, to begin with, there are a lot of options you can put out of your heads as and from this minute!

SHEILA: Well, thank you, Bill—that is very clear now!

BILL: Good.

> *The salon door opens.* MRS. BROPHY *and* MICHAEL *come out. Her hair is very striking in an assortment of curlers.*

MICHAEL: (*Awkwardly*) Sorry, Mum—she said she had to...

BROPHY: I beg your pardon—just need to visit the Little Girl's Room for a moment.

MICHAEL: Sorry, Mum, I couldn't...

BILL: (*Quietly*) Good God.

SHEILA: Alright, Michael. Use the toilet upstairs, Mrs. Brophy—that one is still closed off.

BROPHY: (*Indicates the downstairs toilet*) Oh then, now's your chance to turn it into a little sauna, yes. Be very handy there, yes.

SHEILA: Upstairs, to the left—it has a cream door.

BROPHY: What? Oh, grand, yes. Beg your pardon again. (*To* BILL) How are ya. (*Goes upstairs.*)

MICHAEL: (*Awkwardly*) Hello, Mr. Patterson. (*Is ignored. Goes into the salon.*)

BILL: (*Pause. Quietly*) I really am quite amazed at you, Brendan. We all are. Helen—everyone. Not only is it unsightly and unsuitable and attracting all kinds into the area but, as Helen said last night, it is a totally suicidal business venture. (*Pause*) Beyond me how you approved of it, Brendan.

BRENDAN: (*Quietly*) Well, if you must know, Bill—I never approved of it: not when I first heard it mentioned, not when it was being built and not now.

BILL: (*Quietly*) Yes, well, I suspected that. Helen said that too—said you wouldn't have. (*Pause*) We both knew that if we had a little chat, just you and I, man-to-man, we'd soon sort it out together. And I still think we can.

BRENDAN: I was the first to disapprove, Bill.

BILL: I'm quite sure you were—it's your house valuation too, isn't it? (*Looks at his watch.*)

BRENDAN: I hated it then and I hate it now.

BILL: We all hate it, Brendan. It's an eye-sore and it is an embarrassment. Only yesterday, Helen drove three miles around to some coffee morning because she couldn't bring herself to look at it. It couldn't possibly stay.

BRENDAN: To me, it was going back to everything we had left behind...

BILL: Exactly—and no team wins by doing that. We need to push forward...

BRENDAN: (*Hotly*) I hate it, Bill—but if I were asked to name one thing that I hate more than seeing it there every morning, I'd say seeing the bloody interview boards I sit in front of every morning—looking at them, telling them about my business, my experience, my rugby days, my plans, my contacts, my willingness to work anywhere, for any number of hours—and then hearing them gently remind me of how old I am...and would I ever mind buggering off and annoying someone else.

BILL: Now, Brendan—don't start thinking that way: I told you what Gerry said...

BRENDAN: Right then, Bill, let's get down to details—what exactly did Gerry say? He didn't say he'd give me the job, did he?

BILL: Well, he can't just say: here is a job, here is a business.

BRENDAN: (*Of the Salon*) But I could say there is a job, here is a business.

BILL: It is a business—a business without a future—a gilt-edged failure and you know it!

BRENDAN: But maybe it would work—and that's more definite than anything Gerry could offer me or any interview could promise me or...

BILL: It will never work and you will lose everything by pretending it will. Think of your position, for God's sake.

BRENDAN: (*Collapse*) I am thinking of my position, Bill—and in case you haven't noticed, my position is that I'm a middle-aged redundant executive in a world of young, qualified executives and, Bill, I'm so bloody tired going from interview to interview. I'm tired listening to empty promises and then coming home here to my family and smiling at them and pretending that everything is great, everything is positive...

SHEILA: Brendan...

BRENDAN: I'm tired running around the roads trying to prove that I'm still young enough to run faster than all the other washed-up failures...I'm tired of sticking things in my eyes to make me look younger.

BILL: You are backing off!

BRENDAN: I need a bloody job, Bill—I have a responsibility to my family...

BILL: You're backing off!

BRENDAN: You're telling me about Gerry O'Dowd and all his promises and hope and...

BILL: We all have hope, Brendan—and, by God, hope is better than that thing there.

BRENDAN: The dole? Is the dole better than it? Is it? Is it?

BILL: (*Explodes*) Well, there it is now, Brendan! I knew we'd come to this! You are backing off—you always did that—you always backed off just when you were getting somewhere, you always wanted to lose...

BRENDAN: (*Explodes*) I never backed off! I had the best Agency in Ireland...

BILL: And what happened to it?

BRENDAN: I was the one who used to invite *you* to dinners and conferences and meetings...

BILL: Yes, and you lost it all by backing off...

BRENDAN: I did not—I fought all the way, but the recession...

BILL: You didn't fight—we all told you to diversify and fight but you did nothing and you threw it all away—just as you threw away your rugby career by not fighting, by backing off...

BRENDAN: I did not!

BILL: You did and you know it!

BRENDAN: I was capped for Ireland, for God's sake—there's my international cap hanging on the wall...

BILL: Yes—one cap! You got your one cap and in your one Welsh game, you backed off and they dropped you and that's all it takes: make one mistake and you're finished...

BRENDAN: I was injured in that Welsh game—I had a hair-line fracture...I was in plaster from here...

BILL: You backed off—but you're very lucky, Brendan—you have a
second chance—a chance to put things right. (*More calmly*) Don't
ignore it—don't ruin a good business career for that short-term
bottle of smoke. Show us all that you are a man's man, a fighter
and a survivor—and, for God's sake, get back on the winning
team.

MRS. BROPHY *comes slowly down the stairs.*

BROPHY: Beg your pardon again.

BILL: (*To* BRENDAN) Or is that your idea of a winning team?

BROPHY: Very nice tiling in your bathroom and, I hope you don't mind,
but I peeped in at your built-in wardrobes. A bit of dark stain
would really set them off, yes.

SHEILA: This way, Mrs. Brophy.

BROPHY: Oh right. Sorry to be a nuisance, yes.

SHEILA *and* MRS. BROPHY *go into the salon. The door is
closed,* BILL *relaxes.*

BILL: (*Merrily*) Ah, Brendan—some hard tackling there—a lot of the
shoulder, the occasional knee in the groin, the thumb in the eye,
even—but it's a man's game, well worth it if we can get an old
team-mate back on the right track...and back on the winning
team. (*Pause. Intimately*) There was something else I wanted to
mention before that blew up—hat number three, my main hat, my
French hat. There will, of course, be job creations and parallel
positions here when we get this French agency off the ground—
we'll need the right man for our team—but perhaps we'd better
leave that until I get back—until we get this unfortunate business
sorted out.

SHEILA *has come from the salon. Stands un-noticed.*

BRENDAN: This...this French agency will...will it create positions in
France or...?

BILL: Or here in Dublin, whichever you like. Brendan, I see the French
position as a matter of choice for you.

BRENDAN: Matter of choice?

BILL: Absolutely—(*Pointed*) All things being equal.

BRENDAN: (*Realises*) Oh, I have you now. All things being equal.

BILL: (*Merrily*) Exactly. All right?

BRENDAN: Yes, Bill.

BILL: Good. Excellent. And we have to arrange a pow-wow about Royal
Portrush too—we need to sit down together sometime and select
our team. But now, I must fly—if you will excuse the pun!

BRENDAN: (*Laughs*) Oh yes. Well, thanks very much, Bill. And you'll let me know, I suppose, how the Paris meeting...

BILL: I'll tell you what I'll do: I'll drop in on my way back on Monday: tell you what happened and—all things being equal—perhaps we can have a more positive chat then.

BRENDAN: Grand, Bill—I must say that Paris sounds very interesting.

BILL: Delighted to hear you say that, Brendan. (*Sees* SHEILA) Sheila— lovely to see you again.

SHEILA: Yes, Bill. Our regards to Helen.

BILL: Indeed. And our love to Catherine—and tell Paul to keep at it— he's a winner. See you Monday. (*Goes.*)

BRENDAN: Okay, Bill—and good luck in Paris.

The door closes. Silence.

SHEILA: Well?

BRENDAN: Well what?

SHEILA: Well, what do you want me to do?

BRENDAN: What do I want *you* to do? This is a big departure, isn't it?

SHEILA: It's a bigger departure than you think.

BRENDAN: And what's that supposed to mean?

SHEILA: You've made up your mind, haven't you?

BRENDAN: I've made up my mind that I want a bloody job, yes.

SHEILA: And the Salon?

BRENDAN: Well, you heard what Bill said. He said that we...

SHEILA: (*Angrily*) Right. Well, whatever you say, Brendan. As soon as she leaves, I'll turn off the lights, I'll lock it up, I'll cancel all the bookings and I'll phone the workmen to come first thing Monday to put back your garage. That's what you want, isn't it?

BRENDAN: Well, if we're to have any chance of...

SHEILA: And I'll tell Michael to find himself a new career—and then you can sit here telling jokes about rugby scrums and jock-straps while you wait for Bill Patterson to keep his promises...

BRENDAN: Now, wait a minute...

SHEILA: (*Picks up the glasses*) But you'll be sitting here and telling jokes to yourself, Brendan—because I certainly will not be around to hear them.

BRENDAN: You won't be around where? What the hell are you talking about?

SHEILA: I've had it, Brendan. I've had eighteen months of trying to do something for you—eighteen months of thinking up ways to make this family survive—but no more. So you just tell me what to do now, and I'll do it, and then I'll go.

BRENDAN: Go? Now look here, Sheila, get this into your head: we've just had an offer to start in business right at the very top...

SHEILA: We haven't had an offer to start anywhere—bottom, middle or top...

BRENDAN: (*Angrily*) Then you must have been asleep when Bill talked about Paris...

SHEILA: And you must be blind if you can't see that he is just dangling carrots in front of you...

BRENDAN: (*Desperately*) Don't say that—he is not!

SHEILA: He's turning you this way and that way to get what he wants— and he doesn't give a damn what happens to you...

BRENDAN: Will you shut up—he's offering me a business deal in Paris...

SHEILA: (*Throws down the tray of glasses*) Don't, Brendan! For Christ sake, don't! If you're not going to change, if you're not going to admit that all that business stuff is over for you...

BRENDAN: Of course it isn't over for me!

SHEILA: If you're not going to admit that the past was great and we made it successful and we enjoyed it but now it's gone; if you're not going to tell me that you can now change and build a new future with something that has a future; if you're not going to tell me any of that, then for God's sake, don't tell me anything at all...

BRENDAN: Sheila!

SHEILA: Because I'm sick and tired of the whole thing and I don't care any more and you can go ahead and wreck your life but you can do it on your own—because once that Salon has been demolished, I will be gone to hell out of this house of yours forever...and don't think I won't! (*Runs upstairs.*)

BRENDAN: (*Calls*) Sheila? Sheila, you've got it all wrong. We have been given a second chance—a great chance to get this whole house back to normal. (*The door bell rings*) Things are going to be the same as they once were. It will be the Caribbean, dinners out—I promised you all of that before and I gave it to you, didn't I? Well, this is it again—things are going to be normal again in this house. (*The door bell rings again.* BRENDAN *answers it.* MR. MULLI-GAN—*with two large suitcases—walks in*). Oh God—I spoke too soon!

IMMEDIATE FADE

ACT TWO

Scene Three

Monday morning. MARY *stands looking out the window. She is in her school uniform.* SHEILA *comes from the kitchen—angrily tidying up the rooms. The Salon is closed-up and in darkness.*

SHEILA: It's nearly nine o'clock, Mary—or has your school been closed as well as everything else?

MARY: (*Sharply*) No. Bobby Collins is calling for me.

SHEILA: And when was that arranged?

MARY: Yesterday—when I phoned him.

SHEILA: Hot with the news, weren't you?

MARY: Yes—and we both agreed that our relationship had been need-lessly threatened but Bobby said that now that the Salon is closed we can distance ourselves from the problem and find the real meaning of our relationship and a new awareness of our problems.

SHEILA: He sounds like a raving lunatic. You brought those letters up to Aunt Catherine?

MARY: Yes, she was asleep.

BRENDAN: (*Off*) Sheila, did you see my golf-club tie anywhere?
    SHEILA *ignores this.* MR. MULLIGAN *comes from the kitchen.*

MULLIGAN: Lovely breakfast, Mrs. Ryan.

SHEILA: Thank you, Mr. Mulligan—and I'm sorry I can't give you the room on a...

MULLIGAN: No no, temporary is grand. It's just until I rebuild my stocks and find another lodging place.

BRENDAN: (*Off angrily*) Sheila, I can't see my golf-club tie anywhere.

SHEILA: I hope you're successful, Mr. Mulligan—especially after Cork.

MULLIGAN: Well, thank God I held on to a few legs and arms and elbows—and I didn't give all my money to that Cork chancer. So, I can start again—and I'm thinking of going into skeletons.

SHEILA: That sounds interesting.

MULLIGAN: (*Jokes*) If my new landlady makes no bones about it!
    BRENDAN *comes down the stairs. He is dressed in slacks and an open shirt.*

BRENDAN: For God's sake, Sheila, Bill will be at that door any minute and I can't find my bloody tie anywhere. (*Looks.*)

SHEILA: Well, I'm certainly not wearing it!

MULLIGAN: I can loan you this one, Mr. Ryan—I got it for ceili dancing down in Cork. I bet you're surprised to know that I can do ceili dancing. Look. (*Does a step.*)

BRENDAN: Don't annoy me, Mr. Mulligan. (*Looks around still.*)

MARY: Daddy, I saw a tie on the back of the bathroom door.

MULLIGAN *goes quickly upstairs.*

BRENDAN: Thanks, Mary. (*Sees* MULLIGAN) Excuse me, Mr. Mulligan—where are you galloping off to?

MULLIGAN: (*Stops*) I have some artificial arms and elbows to wash.

BRENDAN: Well, I have some *real* arms and elbows to wash—so if you don't mind. (*Goes up.*)

MULLIGAN: No, not at all. Mine can wait. (*Goes up.*)

A motor-cycle is heard outside.

MARY: (*Excited*) It's Bobby! Hi Bobby. Hi Bobby!

SHEILA: Wear a crash-helmet if you're getting on that motor-bike.

MARY: Bobby is giving me his to keep and he's painted our two names on it so everyone will know. (*Runs out*) Hi Bobby! (*Comes back*) Mummy, Mr. Patterson is driving up. (*Runs out. Off*) Hi, Mr. Patterson!

SHEILA: (*Calls upstairs*) He's here—Bill Patterson is here.

BRENDAN: (*Off*) Sheila, that tie on the back of the bathroom door is the cord from somebody's pyjamas.

SHEILA: I'll be in the kitchen if you want me.

BRENDAN: (*Off*) What? For God's sake, Sheila—talk to Bill for a minute...until I find this tie.

A motor-cycle is heard going off as BILL PATTERSON *appears in the doorway. He carries a bottle of whiskey.*

SHEILA: Come in, Bill. Brendan will be down in a minute.

BILL: I left the car engine running so I won't keep him a minute. Some duty-free for you, Sheila. (*Puts the bottle down.*)

SHEILA: You shouldn't have bothered.

BILL: No bother—the lads in the Customs know me well. I could bring the stuff in in crates!

BRENDAN *comes down the stairs. He wears a cravat.*

BILL: And look at this fellow! Good morning, Brendan.

BRENDAN: Bill, sorry to keep you—I was finishing off that German report.

SHEILA: (*To* BRENDAN) Bill brought you that.

BILL: No, no—for both of you.

BRENDAN: Very kind of you, Bill.

SHEILA *goes into the kitchen.*

BRENDAN: You'll have a brandy? (*Goes to the drinks.*)

BILL: Well, I've left the car running—really thought I'd drop in to see how things were...(*Of the salon*) and I am very glad to see that, Brendan. Very glad.

BRENDAN: Oh, the Salon? Well yes, Sheila and I chatted it over, looked at the pros and cons and the outcome is that we've the workmen coming in this morning to put a garage where a garage should be.

BILL: (*Drinks*) Excellent, Brendan. And very wise—very wise indeed.

BRENDAN: (*Hopefully*) Yes?

BILL: Oh most certainly. I know it wasn't an easy decision—but that will open doors that were being slowly closed on you.

BRENDAN: Well, we chatted it over and felt it was the right thing.

BILL: Absolutely. (*Pause*) And how's Paul's shiner?

BRENDAN: What?

BILL: Paul's eye. Healed up all right?

BRENDAN: Oh yes, I think so. He can take a few knocks and keep coming back.

BILL: Like his old man. (*Of the salon*) And that is excellent. Helen phoned me in Paris, you know—but I told her that Brendan is a team-man. No worries.

BRENDAN: Well, we chatted it over and...

BILL: (*Suddenly*) Great. So I'll be off, Brendan—oh, drop over sometime and we'll select our team for Portrush.

BRENDAN: (*Anxiously*) What? Oh yes. And Paris went all right?

BILL: Paris is very promising, Brendan—very, very promising.

BRENDAN: Oh good. And there'll be an Irish input...?

BILL: Absolutely—and some great ideas, some great concepts being explored there.

BRENDAN: Well, that does sound promising...

BILL: Very promising—good reasons for a lot of optimism. And could you drop in those Caribbean photos for Helen? (*Moves to leave.*)

BRENDAN: What? Oh yes. And when do you think the agency will actually begin?

BILL: Well, early days yet—still rolling the pitch, so to speak.

BRENDAN: Because, Bill—as I said—I find it very attractive and I feel my experience could contribute...

BILL: And I'm delighted to hear you say that because—between you and I—smart young graduates are all very fine but, let's be honest, most of them would have to be shown how to lace up their boots.

BRENDAN: So you think there'll certainly be a position there if I...

BILL: Without a doubt there'll be plenty of positions—a whole new team will have to be picked. (*Moves to go.*)

BRENDAN: Oh, that's great! But when, Bill? I mean, I'd like to know as soon as possible...

BILL: (*Laughs*) And wouldn't we all—but games are not won until the final whistle and now's the time to keep possession, so to speak...

BRENDAN: (*Testily*) I was really hoping, Bill, that you'd have something more definite...

BILL: Absolutely—as soon as we see a gap in the defence...

BRENDAN: You see, I'd prefer Paris to Gerry O'Dowd's offer because of all the interviews and...

BILL: Okay, I'll drop the word about that preference and, as I always say, a word at the right time can send a man clear, around the blind side, up along the touch-line, jigging in and out through the defence, selling the dummy...

BRENDAN: (*Explodes*) For Christ sake, Bill, will you stop all the rugby shit and tell me straight what my bloody position is!

BILL: (*Explodes*) Yes! Alright! I will tell you what your position is before you ask me another million questions. I went to Paris and I stuck my neck out for you and...

BRENDAN: Will I get the job?

BILL: Yes, you will—but you will have to...

BRENDAN: Good. Now when? When will I get it?

BILL: When you've gone through the proper channels.

BRENDAN: What proper channels?

BILL: What proper channels do you think?

BRENDAN: You mean interviews?

BILL: For God's sake, Brendan—you're not a baby—of course I mean interviews.

BRENDAN: Against other candidates.

BILL: Well, hardly against cats and dogs!

BRENDAN: Who are younger than me?

BILL: I don't know what age they are.

BRENDAN: So now we're back to the bloody interview merry-go-round: candidates, applications, waiting, phone calls...

BILL: Now look here—I stuck my neck out for you in Paris—I mentioned your name to them and...

BRENDAN: And what did they say?

BILL: What *could* they say?

BRENDAN: No—what *did* they say?

BILL: They said they were interested...

BRENDAN: Interested? That's all?—interested?

BILL: Well, what did you expect them to say? Did you think that at the mention of your name, they'd jump up on the tables and do the can-can with delight? They don't know who the hell you are or what you did and they'll probably soon find out that you haven't worked for almost two years and they'll want to know why—but, despite that, I stuck my neck out for you and...

BRENDAN: Well you can keep your neck where it is! Sheila was bloody well right about you. (*Shouts*) Michael?

BILL: Now wait a minute, Brendan...

BRENDAN: (*Shouts*) Michael? Where the hell are you? Michael!

BILL: Do you think I enjoyed pleading your case in Paris?

MICHAEL *comes quickly down the stairs.*

MICHAEL: Did you call me, Dad?

BRENDAN: I've been roaring for you at the top of my bloody voice. Open it!

BILL: Now look here, Brendan—I wouldn't advise you to do anything stupid at this sensitive stage...

SHEILA *comes from the kitchen.*

BRENDAN: (*To* MICHAEL) Did you hear me? Open it!

MICHAEL: Open what?

BILL: (*To* MICHAEL) Open nothing, Michael. Now, Brendan, both Helen and I have a lot of...

BRENDAN: To hell with Helen and you. (*To* MICHAEL) Open that blasted place before I break it open!

MICHAEL: I haven't the key, Dad.

BILL: Alright, Brendan—I'll only say this once...

SHEILA: (*To* MICHAEL) The key is on the ledge.

BRENDAN: (*To* MICHAEL) Get the key off the ledge and open that place up.

BILL: Don't touch that key, sonny—don't go near it. (*To* BRENDAN) If you allow that boy to open that...

SHEILA: (*To* MICHAEL) Open it when you're told to open it!

BILL: You stay out of this, Sheila!

BRENDAN: (*To* MICHAEL) Open it!

MICHAEL *runs to the salon, finds the key and opens the door.*

BILL: Brendan, I'm only going to say this once...

BRENDAN: You've said that twice already.

BILL: Then you have good reasons to remember it: if you open that Salon, I will destroy you—I will personally see to it that you never get a job in any worthwhile business in this city...

BRENDAN: (*To* MICHAEL) Turn on the lights.

MICHAEL: Turn on the lights. (*He turns on the lights.*)

BILL: You are on the verge of making the biggest mistake of your life...but you still have a chance, if we'll just talk...

BRENDAN: Turn on the music.

MICHAEL: Turn on the music. (*Turns on the music.*)

BILL: (*Pause*) I never thought you could be so stupid.
The door bell rings.

BRENDAN: Well, now you know.

BILL: And the real stupidity, the great stupidity—the stupidity that hasn't hit you yet but will hit you when it is too late—is that your Salon is doomed to failure.

BRENDAN: It is not doomed to failure.

BILL: And you could have had everything—I'd have got you the Gerry O'Dowd job and, with that, I'd have given you a track-record that would have taken you into the Paris agency...but you didn't want it. You want to be a loser, Brendan—that's your whole trouble. You don't want to win. You're afraid to be a winner.
The door bell rings again. SHEILA *goes quickly to open it to* MR. DAVIS *and* BIMBO. *They carry in sledge-hammers, picks and the roll of plastic sheeting.*

DAVIS: We skipped our breakfast to come as quick as we could—but we're not complaining.

BIMBO: No, we're not complaining...

BRENDAN: Come in, come in.

BILL: (*To* BRENDAN). There's still time. You can still tell them to pull that place down.

DAVIS: (*To* BILL). That's what we're here to do, sir. We skipped a good...

BRENDAN: You're not pulling it down. You're not pulling any place down.

DAVIS: We're not?

BILL: (*To* BRENDAN). Then you're finished. Your whole family is finished. You will not be tolerated in the business world, you will not be tolerated in this neighbourhood—and now you can hang a few hairdressers' combs and brushes there on the wall beside your one miserable cap and your son can forget even getting a place on the *trial* side. Nobody will touch you in this town. You are totally finished. (*Turns to go*).

BRENDAN: Bill? (BILL *stops*). Am I still captain of your golf tour of Royal Portrush?
In fury, BILL *turns and snaps up his bottle of whiskey. Leaves— slamming the door.* MULLIGAN *comes down the stairs. He carries his sales suitcase, some limbs and some account books.*

83

BIMBO: (*To* MULLIGAN). Hey, you're back again.

MULLIGAN: Oh hello—things didn't go well in the butcher's.

BIMBO: The butcher's!

MULLIGAN: So I'm back to start again. Fortunately I kept a few arms and legs—but I'll be very short of knee-caps.

BIMBO: (*To* DAVIS). Hey Da—I think he's looking at you!

DAVIS: He needn't bother looking at me—I'm crippled with arthur-itis.

BRENDAN: (*To* DAVIS) Mr...eh...

SHEILA: Davis.

BRENDAN: Davis. I believe you were asked to come here and turn that into a garage?

DAVIS: Don't tell me—you want a Fish and Chip Shop after all—is that it?

BRENDAN: No, that's not it. I want it left as it is.

DAVIS: You want it left as it is?

BRENDAN: Yes.

DAVIS: So you called us out at this hour of the morning to come over as quickly as we could to leave it as it is?

BRENDAN: Yes.

DAVIS: Well, that's grand. We can do that. We will leave it as it is and we will send you our bill for that. Thank you. (*Turns to leave*).

BRENDAN: But as you're here, perhaps you'd look at the sign outside— see if we could have another, facing the other way.

DAVIS: (*Enthusiastic*) Oh, certainly, sir. We'll be happy to make an assessment of that work and give you an estimate of our charges...

DAVIS–BIMBO: (*Recite together*)...as per our general estimate that would include VAT, materials and labour or as per our special estimate that would be paid in cash and would not require a receipt. (DAVIS *gives* BRENDAN *a knowing wink.*)

BRENDAN: (*Gives* DAVIS *a knowing wink*) If we could have them both and then we will decide.

DAVIS: (*Angrily*) I see, sir. Come on, Bimbo. Ignore everything else. (*Turns to leave.*)

CATHERINE *appears on the stairs. She carries a letter.*

BIMBO: (*To* CATHERINE) Sister, never give the bourgeoisie imperialists an inch. (*Goes.*)

DAVIS: Or a receipt! (*Goes.*)

BRENDAN: Catherine, I suppose I should explain...

CATHERINE: Explain nothing, Brendan. I heard all of that: you have chosen to ignore the advice of Bill Patterson—but your downfall does not concern me anymore. This came in the post. (*Holds up the letter.*)

BRENDAN: What did?

CATHERINE: The woman you all said was a zombie has won the competition.

BRENDAN: Are you serious?

CATHERINE: Of course I'm serious.

SHEILA: You mean you've won the five thousand pounds?

CATHERINE: You stupid woman—I am still doing that competition. I have won the fourteen day tour of the Isle of Man...for two.

BRENDAN: Well, congratulations, Catherine.

CATHERINE: (*Louder*) For two, Mr. Mulligan.

MULLIGAN: Two what, Miss Ryan?

CATHERINE: (*Haughtily*) Mr. Mulligan, if you agree, I'd prefer not to discuss my private affairs in this vulgarly public area. So, would you care to join me in the breakfast room—when you have finished putting your legs together. (*Goes into the kitchen.*)

MULLIGAN: What? Oh, these legs? Right. (*To all*) Excuse me. (*Pauses. Fixes hair. Slightly embarrassed, follows* CATHERINE.)

MICHAEL *goes into the salon where he begins to polish and prepare the place for business.* SHEILA *sits beside* BRENDAN.

BRENDAN: What have I done? What the hell have I done?

SHEILA: You did the right thing.

BRENDAN: You realise, of course, that if that fails, we're really finished—I mean bloody-well wiped out, washed-up, sunk, forgotten.

SHEILA: It won't fail.

BRENDAN: I said that once before and look what happened to me.

SHEILA: (*Takes his hand*) No Brendan, this is different—we're really doing good business...have you seen the register? We shouldn't be thinking of failing, we should be thinking of extending.

BRENDAN: Extending?!

SHEILA: We have to believe that, if we want to succeed.

The phone rings.

BRENDAN: I'll get that. (*Rises. Stops. Pause*) If that is for an interview, I'm turning it down. No matter what they say, I'm turning it down. Alright?

SHEILA: Right. (*Croses her fingers in hope.*)

BRENDAN: Right. (*Lifts the phone*) Brendan Ryan speaking. (*Pause. Decides. Brightly*) Yes, madam, that's right: this is Hairstyling by Michel! (*Calls*) Michel! It's for you!

The salon music is clear: as MICHAEL *comes from the salon, as* SHEILA *holds* BRENDAN, *as curtain slowly falls.*

BERNARD FARRELL

Born in Sandycove, Co. Dublin, Bernard Farrell spent sixteen years working for Sealink while he wrote regular features for Dublin's *Evening Press*, poetry for various periodicals and had his short stories included in *The Anthology of Irish Writing*. However, after the success of his first play I DO NOT LIKE THEE, DOCTOR FELL at the Abbey Theatre in 1979, he resigned his job to write full-time for the theatre.

Since then, most of his plays have been premiered at the Abbey and have later been produced in the USA, Canada, UK, Belgium, Germany and Australia. His second Abbey play was CANARIES for which he was awarded the 1980 Rooney Prize for Irish Literature. This was followed in 1981 by ALL IN FAVOUR SAID NO! which, after its Abbey run, opened at the South Coast Repertory Theatre in Los Angeles. His adaptation of a Dion Boucicault play, PETTY SESSIONS, was the Abbey's Christmas 1983 presentation and this was followed by his adaptation of Moliere's DON JUAN at the Peacock. In 1985 his ALL THE WAY BACK was premiered and later revived at the Abbey. In 1987 his SAY CHEESE! enjoyed an extended nine-week run.

He has been Writer-in-Residence for TEAM Theatre-in-Education Company and with them wrote THEN MOSES MET MARCONI (1984), ONE-TWO-THREE-O'LEARY (from Grips Berlin, 1985) and BECAUSE JUST BECAUSE (1986). For Moving Theatre he wrote LEGS ELEVEN and later adapted this play for television.

He has also written a number of radio plays including GLIDING WITH MR. GLEESON (BBC and RTE), THE SCHOLARSHIP TRIO (RTE), THE YEAR OF JIMMY SOMERS (RTE entry for the 1987 *Prix Italia*) and MR. HEGARTY'S HEN HOUSE (BBC).

Bernard Farrell's television work includes LOTTY COYLE LOVES BUDDY HOLLY (RTE 1988) and, with Graham Reid, three series of FOREIGN BODIES for BBC2.

He has also adapted his Abbey play SAY CHEESE! for RTE television. With Ulick O'Connor, he completed a play on Brendan Behan entitled MY LAUGHING BOY.

Bernard Farrell is married and lives in Greystones, Co. Wicklow.

MASTERS OF IRISH THEATRE

This major new series presents in a uniform format the very best of 20th century Irish drama. Each volume contains an important Irish play, complete with a substantial introduction to the work by the playwright.

VOLUME 1
THE MASK OF MORIARTY
HUGH LEONARD

The definitive text of this theatrical success is complemented by a lengthy diary in which playwright Leonard chronicles the conception, writing and rewriting of **The Mask of Moriarty**. Hugh Leonard says of the Dairy:
"It was embarked on as a private diary...I wanted, for the first time, to set down the early history of a play, from conception to the point during rehearsals where the author lets go of its hand and allows it to walk unaided..."
ISBN: 0 907960 83 9   **Price: IR£5.95.**

VOLUME 2
MADIGAN'S LOCK and PIZZAZZ
HUGH LEONARD

Madigan's Lock was revived at the Abbey for the 1987 Dublin Theatre Festival, having been first staged at the Gate Theatre in Dublin in 1958. **Pizzazz**, an elegantly-crafted One-Act play, was first performed at Dublin's Olympia Theatre in 1984.
ISBN: 0 0907960 88 X   **Price: IR£5.95.**

VOLUME 3
SUMMER
HUGH LEONARD

Summer was first produced at the 1974 Dublin Theatre Festival.
ISBN: 1 85405 000 1   **Price: £IR£5.95.**

VOLUME 4
I DO NOT LIKE THEE, DR. FELL
BERNARD FARRELL

I Do Not Like Thee, Dr. Fell was first performed at the Peacock Theatre on 15 March 1979 and transferred to the Abbey Theatre in November 1979.
ISBN 0 907960 94 4   **Price: IR£5.95.**

VOLUME 5
ALL THE WAY BACK
BERNARD FARRELL

All the Way Back was first performed at the Abbey Theatre on 14 March 1985. It returned to the Abbey on 29 July 1985 for the summer season.
ISBN: 0 907960 99 5   **Price: IR£5.95.**

BROPHY BOOKS
**108 SUNDRIVE ROAD
DUBLIN 12 • IRELAND
Telephone (01) 971617 and (01) 973061**